Craft of Counter Insurgency

Customized Response and Tactical Tips for the Frontline

Attention Authors

Manas Publications is fighting a war to tell the world that India can win the battle not only by the bullet but also by pen. There is no dearth of intellectuals in our country, but their knowledge is confined to them only. No sincere effort has been made by any other publisher to channelise their knowledge in national interest, which is why the talent of large number of intellectuals remain latent. An author always gives the raw material in the shape of a manuscript and it is the job of the publisher to convert it to a beautiful book. Manas always motivates the intellectuals by publishing their manuscripts since more than four decades and would like to publish your manuscript too. If you or your colleagues have any manuscript ready for publication or are working on it, kindly contact us with a detailed synopsis and list of contents for its best publication. If you wish, we can also suggest you a suitable title for writing related to your area of expertise. Manas is known for its publishing quality and commitments. We take utmost care in production and give wide publicity to the book as well as its author through our national and international distribution network.

Craft of Counter Insurgency

Customized Response and Tactical Tips for the Frontline

Dr AP Maheshwari
(Indian Police Service) IPS

Manas Publications
(We Convert Fighters into Writers)
New Delhi-110002 (INDIA)

MANAS PUBLICATIONS
(Publishers, Library Suppliers, Importers & Exporters)
4402/5-A, Ansari Road (Opp. HDFC Bank)
Darya Ganj, New Delhi-110 002 (India)
Off. ✆ 23260783, 23265523, Res. ✆ 23842660
Fax: 011-23272766
E-mail: manaspublications@vsnl.com
manaspublications@yahoo.com
manaspublications@gmail.com

ISBN 978-81-7049-413-3
₹ 695/-

Designed at
Manas Publications

Printed in India at
IYN Graphics, Delhi
and published by Mrs Suman Lata for
Manas Publications, 4402/5-A, Ansari Road
(Opp. HDFC Bank),
Darya Ganj, New Delhi-110 002 (INDIA)

DISCLAIMER

This book contains professional perspectives gathered as a result of various interactions, field experiences and from notes on the subject. It is my fond hope that they will benefit the commanding officers and fine tune their operational skills in the field.

Nothing in this publication amounts to an official stand on any matter, whatsoever.

Views expressed in this book are the author's own and not those of the government.

Dedicated to
my mother late Kamla Devi
who left for her heavenly abode on July 6, 2010

CONTENTS

ACKNOWLEDGEMENTS

I acknowledge the fact that interdependence is better than dependence. I, therefore, owe my gratitude to:

- All those who have been directly or indirectly associated with me and made a lasting impact on my thoughts and deeds.
- My father, Shri Prem Sukh Maheshwari has always taught me how to remain focused and consistent in life. His blessings are reflected in my present work.
- My daughter Shreya who is responsible for egging me on to the successful completion of this book.
- My son Adhar, who inadvertently reinforced my thoughts with his mission statement, 'one should nurture and enjoy those facets of life that grant creative expression to one's inner-self'.
- My sister Vandana who deserves appreciation for boosting my morale and providing expressions

wherever I fell short. Also my brother-in-law Akhileshji who has been constantly supportive in all my endeavours.

- My role model in service, who gave me insight into the dynamics of professional life, in particular Shri Tilak Kak (retd DG, SSB), Shri JK Sinha (retd DG, CRPF), Shri Gopal Sharma (retd DG, J&K), Shri Karmveer Singh (DGP, UP), Shri Nechal Sandhu (Director, Intelligence Bureau) and General VK Singh (Chief of the Army Staff) with whom I had the privilege of working very closely in exacting situations.

I am also thankful to Rinku Das, Maurice and Dileep who provided scripting assistance to me despite their busy schedule.

—Dr AP Maheshwari

FOREWORD

Insurgency is an armed struggle by a group of dissatisfied people against a legitimate government of the state, normally characterised by the presence of a 'Violent Non-State Actor' against the state. Such struggles often involve unconventional warfare, wherein the weaker organisations attempt to use strategies and tactics to offset deficiency in quantity and quality. The manifestations of 'Insurgency' are spread across the domains of militancy, terrorism, guerrilla warfare, low intensity conflict and proxy war.

Today, insurgency is at the centrestage of security concerns of India. The situation in Jammu and Kashmir and the North Eastern states has been witness to a procrastinated array of activities. The Left Wing extremism has further accentuated the agenda with its alarming levels of proliferation into a large number of states. The cross border linkages of insurgent groups and the new paradigms of threat from terrorist organisations are formidable challenges. It entails a multi-dimensional and multi-pronged approach where security forces play a pivotal role in an extremely challenging environment.

AP Maheshwari has made a deep insight into the intrigues of insurgency in Assam in his earlier book titled 'The Folds of Insurgency'. In the present book, the author has deliberated upon the larger canvas wherein he has given a comprehensive description of all insurgencies in India, along with a brief of Naxalism. The realm of all forms of insurgencies is generally long term derivative of faultlines in the socio-economic canvas, poverty and deprivations amongst the masses. The contours of current and future trends of terrorism traced by the author are pragmatic, which provide an insight into the serious security connotations in the new order. The author has rightly put forth his views that counter insurgency should be people centric with assurance of a secure government. This entails a fine balance of governance, development, security and adaptability to maintain the requisite equilibrium in meeting the counter insurgency challenges.

The path of 'Capability Building' should be aimed at strengthening core competencies based on an integrated system's approach. This entails a systematic integration of human aspects with tactical and technical facets. The author's suggestion to focus on human resource aspects by structural reconfiguration of organizations, logistics, training, technology and inorganic areas meritorious. He assigns suitable prudence to mechanisms for creation of automatic response capability. The forces operating on ground are a direct interface of the State with the populace as the prime focus. Therefore, apart from proficiency in tactical and technical skills, he has correctly reiterated that the security forces personnel also have to be trained to ensure a high level of emotional stability and behavioural sensitivity to achieve a high order of personal and collective stress capability. This is critical to operational dynamics in 'Sit Specific Response' mechanism and crisis management.

The author has explored the core aspects of operational dynamics of employment of security forces in CI ops. The operational preparedness has to be based on proactive vision supported by a good 'Intelligence System'. There is a need to develop 'Soft Power' in terms of effective human and electronic surveillance mechanism with an emphasis on a sound database. He has emphasised that the engagements in terms of 'Public Interface' and 'Perception Management' need to be executed with local populace as the centre of gravity. The aspect of winning hearts and minds of people will have to be taken as the prime coefficient of operational success.

The book sketches the counter insurgency scenario, its nuances and response mechanism in a comprehensive format, thereby making it accessible and relevant to the leaders operating in insurgency areas. The ethos of the contents draw our minds back to the basics, which is critically essential for a balanced approach in meeting the security related challenges in counter insurgency environment. The guidelines, procedures and key areas of concern deliberated upon in the book are based on case studies, coupled with vast and varied experience of the author in the North East and J&K. The author has taken pains to explain, at length, the population centric approach, the need to carry human terrain mapping and to understand the power of perception in an insurgency environment.

The author has aptly pointed out that management of change and the sustenance of synergetic response models, covering security related apparatus, hinge upon availability of good intelligence. In addition, there is a need for proactive, cohesive and well integrated leadership with a visionary approach. The changes in technology and the changes in the sub-conventional threats present an ever evolving insurgency environment. It is, therefore, imperative to be innovative and visionary to face emerging challenges. I am sanguine that this book is an apt reading material for the Commanders in all security forces operating across varied forms of insurgencies in the country. This book presents for them a model to comprehend and emulate.

Lt Gen VK Ahluwalia

AVSM**, YSM, VSM

GOC-in-C Central Command,

Lucknow.

INITIATION

"Facts are stubborn things, but statistics are more pliable".

—Mark Twain

I

Encountering insurgency as a part of asymmetric or sub conventional warfare on a low intensity conflict grid calls for dynamic responses which no longer hover around any fixed doctrine. Whereas terror designers have gone far ahead in what we understand now as 'Customized Terror', state sponsored 'switch button' terrorism has simultaneously come under heavy scanners. The new brand of terrorism, supported by legitimacy perceptions that are flowing out of non-linear stratifications, is increasingly gaining ground. It is now prominently political, rather than religious or cultural. While there is no silver bullet to neutralize the monster, this book purports to suggest certain micro modules for security forces in managing low intensity conflicts. These modules have their genesis in the truth that has survived tests in the field amidst various myths.

Various 'circles of hate' around the world seem to nurture terrorism as a social defence, wherein institutionalized formats are operating seamlessly, well networked through a neo breed of ideologically manipulated, glamorized and high profile 'open ground workers'. Under such a scenario one must look for a cause-analysis without being a victim of particularization. One must defeat the doctrine of violence before it is accredited, not sparing even state sponsored violence or the bureaucratized anti-terrorism apparatus. This is what most responsible, concerned citizens feel, as is amply evident from counter radicalization at the level of the nongovernmental organizations.

Victory against the terrorist is different from victory against terrorism. This notion of certain experts needs to be given the due attention it deserves. It will suffice to say at this juncture that security forces alone cannot handle terrorism. The difference between myth and reality on this count shall suo motto evaporate the moment we can differentiate between the telescopic and the microscopic facets of terrorism. That is why we see security and development as the flip sides of the same coin. These are seemingly two different things, but are in fact one. We must be sure of what we need in the end and what we covet before the beginning of that end.

While we carry a risk analysis, threat from terrorism per se doesn't constitute the risk. Secondly, their violent manifestations notwithstanding, displacements and distortions amidst conflicts have become a way of life. What really constitutes the risk is the 'response capability deficit' in optimally foreseeing and proactively handling imminent outbursts. We need not build reactive systems to tackle terrorism, which would generate a perception of 'privileged violence'. In fact, much depends upon how we negotiate the conflict zone.

Some experts feel that under the political federalization, there has been a systematic denigration of the security forces and the police apparatus. Policing experiments in Punjab, Tripura and Andhra Pradesh clearly depict the truth that it is not a case of police incompetency but the lack of 'capacity' given to them which determines the 'difference' this agency can make. Hence, it is crucial to evaluate what are the response deficits of the forces and why over a period of time systematic distortions have changed the intrinsics of a professional response to terrorism. In this context, it won't be out of place to go through some of the observations of analysts like Allen Bruer from France whom I have had the good fortune of hearing in one of the seminars:

- We want things to be what we want them to be.
- We love to solve a problem without analyzing it.
- We love to form a list and then look for the people of that profile.
- To hide our ignorance we claim secrecy.
- To hide incapability we demand resources.
- To hide failure we give global excuses.
- We want to fish where we want to fish and not where the fish abound.

How are we responding to the increasing terrorism:

- Making more rules and Standard Operating Procedures (SOPs)?
- Using more security personnel?
- Using brutal force or draconian laws?

- The question still remains open to debate - will that work?

The experts feel that the highly oscillating vectors of terrorism call for a dynamic response on a constant basis. Transparent responses and open interactions constitute an effective medium. Security forces must learn how to handle partners including the civilians in order to sustain amidst collaborative formats. They must realize the importance of Human Terrain Mapping and seek solutions through community based response models. A capability for a proper diagnosis and generation of operational intelligence will definitely give it an edge. But that too is 'big game' and one has to play it well. There are no set rules. However, we may glance through the following dictums:

- One must see which way the wind is blowing. One must observe the 'games' being played in a given 'wind zone'. Accordingly, make a move to reach a win-win situation.
- Under certain circumstances, one can successfully exploit the weaker links as it is the most flexible and easily pliable. The success in such matters defies the traditional dictum of …'a chain is as strong as its weakest link'.
- One may like to appreciate the difference between an armed response and a more civilian friendly police response in such cases.
- When we can eliminate what is impossible, the remaining then is all possible.

II

There cannot be any permanent policy of 'being defensive'. More often than not, 'offensive postures' have to be resorted to in a well calibrated manner. People, perhaps

organisation's 'operations branch', have provided varied insights time and again. Such experiences tend to reach metamorphosis when exposed to the harsh truth at the ground level.

—*The Author*

CHAPTER 1

PARADIGMS OF LOW INTENSITY CONFLICTS

"There is no security on earth, there is only opportunity".

—General Douglas Mac Arthur

In order to effectively deal with situations of low intensity conflicts and to restore peace along with a fair amount of stability, it is imperative to glance through the dynamics of such conflicts and the wide spectrum within which various stakeholders interact in a conflict situation. The modus operandi may differ in each segment of the conflict spectrum.

Conflict Dynamics

The dynamics of conflict have their genesis in the varied levels of stratifications that may exist on the socio-economic, religio-cultural or the politico-economic grids.

The emerging gaps are vehemently exploited to agitate particular segments. One may find the state as well as the non-state actors on these grids perpetuating their visible as well as invisible agendas. Social life may be paralysed on account of volatile protest behavior, gradually leading to a situation of extreme disorder. Asymmetrical battle spaces may be created where organized crime in the form of trafficking in drugs, illegal weapons, fake currency, money laundering find their way to finance the well calibrated terror onslaughts. With the increasing globalization and enhanced use of modern technologies, all 'Lines of Control' have virtually become porous. It may, therefore, be difficult to zero down on the epicenter.

The conflict spectrum may range from militancy to insurgency and further from proxy war to terrorism. They are making use of indigenous perpetrators, misguided youth, recycled old hands or foreign players introduced on the local conflict grids. One must not miss the point that the centre of gravity is the local population. Whereas terrorists may resort to sensational attacks for mass control, the doctrine of minimum use of force controls the response of the state authorities. This is where the difference between conventional and non-conventional warfare becomes more glaring. The former may be guided by the spirit of destruction, whereas the latter lays emphasis on civil control. The approach is people centric and not area centric. Hence, human rights safeguards, along with a need for minimum collateral damages, guide the actions of the state forces in asymmetrical warfare. Asymmetry has to be understood in terms of application of force versus generation of violence. With the UN conventions, the networking of leading Nations and Nuclear deterrence, full scale conventional wars may be a rare possibility. One would then have to frequently face the asymmetrical, guerilla-like war situations. Under such circumstances, the response pattern of the state could be as under:

Chart - 1

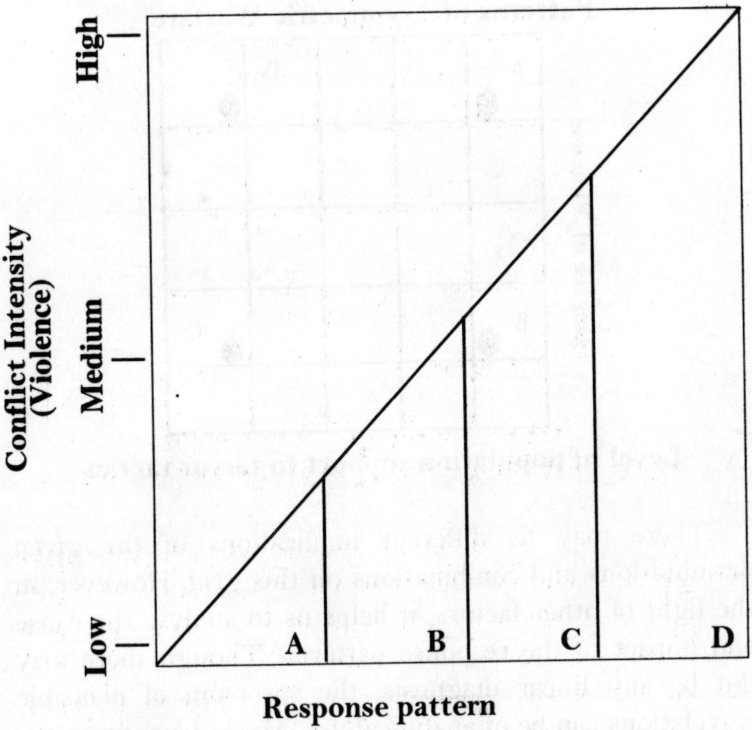

Response pattern of the State

A = Response by local police

B = Response by local police and paramilitary forces

C = Response by local police and army

D = Exclusive response by army

It is emphasised, for the sake of conceptual clarity, that response of the state has to be congruent with the level of violence. This shows the criticality of the transition from situation A to D. The local populace, being the centre of gravity, makes it imperative for the state players to follow the healthy principles of civic control. Hence, there is an increasing reliance on Human Terrain Mapping.

Chart - 2

Patterns of Asymmetric Warfare

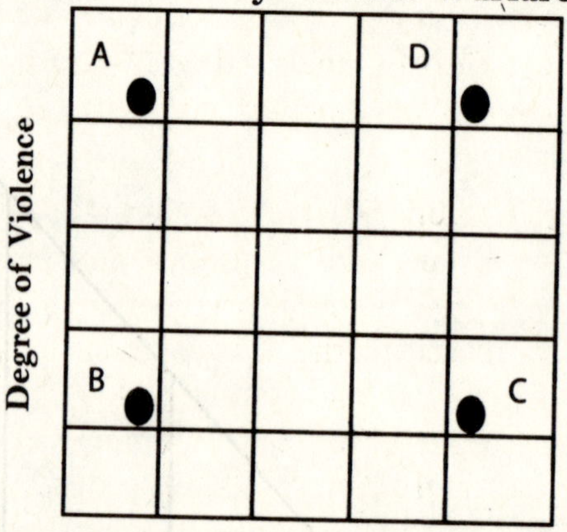

Level of population support to terror tactics

There may be different implications of the given permutations and combinations on this grid. However, in the light of other factors, it helps us to analyse the cause and impact of the response patterns. Though there may not be any linear diagnosis, the spectrum of plausible correlations can be of analytical use. Much depends on the stratifications inbuilt in the Human Terrain. Politically motivated movements may have their epicentre in urban areas, targeting for higher publicity quotients. In contrast, the hinterland may witness insurgencies amidst socio-economic stress despite its low publicity value. At the lower level of the grid, militants may easily emerge as saviours while at higher stages, they may have to 'manipulate' the public perception to emerge as saviours. Going back to the grid, situation 'A' could be indicative of selective intrusion of well trained terror perpetrators to generate a high level of violence, even though the public support is low. In contrast, situation 'D' could indicate a shift of militancy from selective perpetrators to indigenous modules, using the local support bases.

Situation 'C' and 'D' could mean a lack of proper leadership amongst the perpetrators. It could also indicate a 'lull before the storm' situation, in case there are other reasons that are suggestive of hidden potential. These situations could also be analysed by authorities in terms of the response mechanism they configure to counter the onslaught of terror.

At this juncture one must also understand the intricacies of asymmetric warfare and its implicit concerns. The very concept of the front and rear or the flanks disappears in such a war, compared to the conventional battlefield. The difference between strategic and tactical levels is also weaned away and both appear to be coinciding. The difference between a group and the individual becomes insignificant in operational terms. Psychological operations, inter alia, perception management become crucial to generate a 'virtual fighting base'.

Amidst such dynamics, the spill over effect and the 'degree of external linkages' tend to become transnational for various reasons, most important being the need for arms, tactics, money and the OGW (Open Ground Workers) support. This could be followed by the need for hideouts and training bases across the political boundaries. When we talk of OGWs, it could again be seen in terms of individuals, elite groups and the politically or ideologically nurtured frontal organizations.

The oscillating situations of the civic authorities losing their grip, receiving intermittent setbacks, regearing with an enhanced response to restore control through armed intervention may continue with varying degrees of success. Eventually, the state policy and strategy must have multilateral collaborations to generate synergetic effects. What is imperative is to recreate a conducive environment for fulfilling the aspirations of the masses in a democratic way. With this basic understanding, we may now proceed to conduct 'terror profiling', particularly with reference to the Indian sub-continent.

Terror Profiling

In today's world where time and space limitations have been eliminated by globally networked, real-time technological options, any exercise in delineating or ascertaining the profile of various terror groups may, prima-facie, appear to be futile. Tactically, it pays to conduct enemy's SWOT (strength, weakness, opportunity and threat) analysis for which a proper profile needs to be developed. As things extrinsically tend to appear more and more congruent, intrinsically they nurture incoherence. This hypothesis may be more relevant for the analysis of terror modules, given the hidden agenda of the remote players who are managing the show and calibrating the level of violence. Not going into the historical perspectives and the varied views on the genesis and development of terror modules in various pockets of the Indian subcontinent, we may just zero down upon the perceptional specifics of the terror spectrum.

Communally inspired insurgencies are seemingly on the decline. Cultural, religious and economic domains, marred by various particularisations and stratifications have become the breeding ground for terrorism. State as well as non-state players have joined the fray. As observed from various quarters, the technologically exported global terrorism has made deep footprints in the South Asian region. Weapons of mass destruction with remote controlled trigger points and cyber-networked 'information warfare' have made asymmetric warfare more complex and potent. Proliferation through tactics like illegal immigration, smuggling of arms and drugs, circulation of counterfeit currency and money laundering erodes the 'national synergy' levels and impedes all initiatives towards national consolidation. Psychological warfare through perception management and emotional exploitation proves far more effective than the war of guns. Taking advantage of various publicity avenues, politically inspired insurgencies may have their genesis in urban areas. On the contrary, socio-economic stratifications are manipulated to trigger extreme protest behaviour close to terrorism in deprived and backward areas. The terror dynamics also indicate the capability of guerrilla terror groups to strike anywhere at will, keeping the element of surprise with them. These aspects are crucial and need minute study in order to devise proper counter offensives.

Amidst above environmental trends, it would not be out of place to glance through the basic issues in the distinct conflict theatres in the country - J&K, North East, areas infested by Maoist violence, mainland grids affected by Jehadi modules and auxilliary communal as well as criminal networks supporting such modules.

1. Jammu and Kashmir

The geographical and demographic composition of J&K state has undergone drastic changes since 1947-48. Historical events have also altered its contours. Thus, certain areas have come under the occupation of Pakistan and China and a large segment annexed to India under a special treaty. The present conflict situation has its partial genesis in historical events. The issue of plebiscite was also raised before the UN Security Council. However, owing to various diplomatic moves on either side over a period of time, the then passed resolution has seemingly become untenable. This has also been followed by various allegations and counter allegations. The state of J&K has a separate constitution with a special status. The political sub optima have led to civilian discontentment over a period of time. Civilian discontentment has been channelized into armed struggle by the vested interests which have resulted in the formation of separatist organizations. The era of 1989-93 witnessed proxy war through indigenous Kashmiri organizations sponsoring terrorism. Since 1993-99 the presence of foreign mercenaries has also been observed in this state. Thereafter, the simultaneous spread of Jehadi terrorism across the rest of the country has been noticed with the aid of Pakistan based sponsors. Various oscillations and resultant responses, right from public protests to militancy outbursts, have been witnessed. As per the personal assessment and experience of various functionaries in the field, gathered from time to time through informal interactions, the following trends have been observed. These trends depict a swing in the modus-operandi of terror sponsors over a period of time which reflects on their ulterior operational moves. In the absence of any authoritative data to the contrary, some reliance can be placed on them:

- Separatist organizations propounding "Kashmiriyat" and building militant base through indoctrination and armed training were supported by the Pakistan based sponsors under the garb of Islamic Nationalism, giving rise to various militant outfits. This weakened the indigenous organizations. The influx of foreign mercenaries dominated the show in mid 90s. A few organisations were mooted to enforce an orthodox Islamic life style.
- Militancy gradually shifted from the valley to the Jammu region. This was also clubbed with the Jihadi version of indoctrinated militants who had no qualms about ethnic cleansing of the state. It led to a new trend of massacre of the minority groups.
- The impact of militancy has been mostly felt by civilians in terms of human casualties, refugee situations and economic stagnation including a setback to tourism. Narco-trafficking has slowly engulfed the younger generation.
- Muslims, the majority community, have in fact suffered the most as against the general perception that the major brunt was taken by the minority. This

probably was based on the media image following the incidents of minority massacres.

- There has been a gradual shift from selective killings to generating an overall atmosphere of terror. This has been reflected in the modus operandi of a shift from the direct attack to guerilla attacks, car bombs and suicide bombers. Explosive devices have advanced from electric detonators to timers, multi-digit remote controlled mechanism to mobile-triggered circuits. Upgraded acquisitions have also been made in the field of communication, including cyber network. Similarly, OGW support structure and frontal organizations underwent an upwardly change. Infiltration trends have also depicted a well calibrated strategy in this regard so that a minimum level of violence could be maintained. Various indigenous and foreign based militant groups networked to multiply their technical expertise, human resources and funds.
- With the international attention and the will to control terrorism across the globe, growing indigenisation of terror modules has been resorted to. This is also to take advantage of the deniability options and yet keep the conflict grid alive. Attempts have also been made to provide a mass public protest cover to militancy.
- The strategy of excessive reliance on the security forces was replaced by political processes, goodwill missions, peace initiatives and socio-economic development.
- Over a period of time many stakeholders have entered the fray firmly entrenching themselves and making their roots strong. Strategic interests notwithstanding, certain elements are believed

to have converted insurgency into a profitable enterprise.

2. North East

Insurgency in all the seven states of the northeast, hovers around fractured violence between various tribal groups. Only a very small segment of the border of these states is attached with the rest of the Indian states while substantially facing the foreign terrain. Consequently, the insurgent groups with tacit support from their mentors in the neighbourhood countries like Bangladesh, Myanmar, Bhutan and Nepal have come under a heavy scanner of trans-border intelligence agencies. They seem to enjoy the benefit of a safe sanctuary in the border areas along with their training bases. Demographic invasion has led to erosion of the social base and conversion of insurgency to terrorism. Trust deficit has also led to the emergence of new outfits having symbiotic relations with legitimate power structures. Over a period of time, these corridors are being used for smuggling of arms, narcotics and counterfeit currency. Reports from various quarters suggest the presence of extended bases in southeast Asian countries via the sea route, besides bases in the immediate neighbourhood. Interestingly, continuation of chicken-neck connectivity via two percent of land route inter-se northeastern states and the rest of India is of crucial importance. Air route being a costly alternative, these states have no option but to 'look west', in case land connectivity is disturbed. Demographic intrusions have also systematically taken place in this area and certain pockets are now seen to be infested with the Jehadi elements. Authorities have now taken steps to seal the international borders and introduce the system of surveillance. Owing to the neglect of these areas, some experts feel that there has been a loss of 'social resonance' to militancy. Certain groups have been brought under the negotiation mode but core groups and their main members are still at large. The terms of settlement are often flouted. The authorities are still skeptical on adopting harder options. Kidnappings and extortions are still rampant in a few places. Sporadic attacks on security forces as well as civilians continue unabated in some states. The insurgent groups are now techno savvy and use advanced improvised devices following the low cost, high impact options. The geographical terrain provides them with a natural cover for ambushing the security forces. Besides the problems of local adaptability on the part of the security forces that come from outside, the linguistic and cultural barriers tend to further hamper their operational responses. A war of perceptions becoming stronger, the lack of economic development and a state of deprivation of the local inhabitants have become contentious issues to raise the bogey of autonomy and self determination. Alleged atrocities by security forces and other human rights issues are also being propagated as brutal excesses, on the part of the ruling elite. On the other side, the lavish life style of self-exiled leaders of various insurgent outfits and their pursuits to create assets abroad are cited before the masses, exposing the pseudo agenda of such outfits. At times, an oscillating networking of various ultra groups can be seen hinging between convenience and opportunism. Major groups have, however, grown systematically, following proper political and military norms to develop their respective wings. They have been inciting the youth and the students to carry forward their missions. They have established proper funding channels, including the imposition of private levy.

3. Maoist Violence

Not touching upon the historical issues of Naxalism, which gained its name from an initial movement in Naxalbari in West Bengal, it would suffice to focus on the left wing extremism since the formation of CPI (Maoist) in September, 2004, consequent to the merger of CPI(ML),

Peoples War Group and MCCI. Maoists have a systematic modus operandi to ensure area domination. It starts with the identification of the local issues, penetration into the local population base, supporting prevalent issues towards proper resolution, organising people at the cutting edge level in form of 'dalams', and gradually training them for the armed struggle at an opportune moment. To be precise, it means creation of guerilla zones, securing liberated areas and making necessary advances towards capturing the political power. They are gradually moving towards militarization. Capacity building is being done not merely for guerilla warfare in the rural areas, but also to augment mobile warfare potential in urban areas. They have espoused the causes of farmers, backward classes, tribals, women and the minorities. Maoists have reportedly been networking with other groups for enhancing their tactics, weaponary, technologies and financial resources. They also have indigenous capabilities to produce sophisticated weapons. Their training, tactics and drills are well rehearsed and properly documented. An inbuilt audit system of all the actions and happenings induces real time learning for betterment of tactics. Maoists have well networked frontal organizations to espouse their cause in all the main spheres of society including the media and the judicial apparatus. Maoists have well established bases in the areas demarcated by them. Their organizations have central, regional and sub regional committees in the political as well as military arenas. Tactical dexterity gained by Naxals in operational attacks, viz., laying ambush, using wired mines, claymore mines, pressure bombs and harnessing improvised devices is worth being studied. They also derive an advantage from the local terrain. Levy, extortion, donations and other contributions remain a source of their funding. 'Guess-estimates' range upto Rs. 400-600 crores p.a. Owing to good networking and a close assimilation with the intellectual class, Maoist cadres are generally well versed. They are making the best use of available means in the field of engineering as well as communication while devising their operational plans.

The principal objective of CPM (Maoist) appears to be the creation of a Compact Revolutionary Zone (CRZ) right from Andhra Pradesh to Nepal, encompassing Jharkhand, Bihar, West Bengal, Chattisgarh, U.P. and Uttrakhand in this corridor. With the support of Maoist revolutionary organizations an international forum styled as 'the Coordination Committee of Marxist parties of the organization of South Asia' has also been floated with a view to make South Asia an epicenter for the world revolution. It is learnt that Maoists are also networking with NE groups and Jehadis for various purposes under their charter to support the right of self determination by all the ethnic groups and minority segments. On the international forum it is believed that they have effective networking with the Communist Party of Nepal (Maoist), Communist Party of Philippines, Communist Party of Turkey and other like minded parties of the world. Left wing extremism is thriving in the areas that are marred by "developmental and governance" deficit, mainly land reforms and corresponding entitlements. Once Maoists dominate an area, it is difficult for the governance apparatus to function until proper law and order is restored. A lack of adequate infrastructure incapacitates the outside forces in successfully reaching out and neutralizing the hold of the adversaries. Maoists take advantage of such tradeoffs and develop safe operational bases. 'Abhujmad' is one such core area. In urban areas, they tend to make their bases amongst the marginalized segments. Various urban groups and intelligentia are also known to be associated through frontal organizations like PDFI(People's Democratic Front of India).

4. Other Grids

The Jehadi outfits have developed their indigenous bases in the mainland, in addition to the active modules operating in the hinterland. Punjab, UP, Bihar, Maharashtra, Gujarat, Karnataka, Tamil Nadu, Kerala and some of the other states have already witnessed terrorist violence. 'Coastal area' infiltration has been the next move as J&K, Punjab and Rajasthan borders have been properly secured by the Indian Forces. Land routes through neighbouring countries are also being exploited, taking advantage of the existing friendly ties between the nations. Mutual apprehensions have also brought various intelligence agencies into the fray giving rise to virtual warfare through "sources" that have their own game plans.

There have also been strong indications, besides the inferential happenings, that suggest a positive correlation between the Jehadi modules and the Communal operatives. Some observers even perceive the presence of common local cells, working on both the axis, for monetary gains or for the sake of indoctrination. Psychological warfare through perception management has been in vogue in the communally sensitive towns. OGW support systems are also deemed to be in place. Frontal organizations like PFI(Popular Front of India) have been alleged to be associated with terror modules.

At this juncture, it may also be relevant to take into account the impact of the new generation crimes on terrorism and vice-versa. Right from technologically enabled crime through programmed codes, we may go on to technologically facilitated crimes in the virtual as well as the real world, more so the crimes related to life style changes or crimes having their genesis in globalization and corporate work culture. The economic or cultural crimes are no less pertinent if we were to go deep into the investigative trails. Crimes involving human trafficking, organ trade, fake currency, environmental degradations, drugs and narcotics are found to have been perpetuated by 'common terror modules'.

Thus, asymmetric warfare domains are multifaceted. What we generally see are the overt domains. The more dangerous and deeper area of concern is the 'zone of covert operations'. With globalization, various economic, cultural and educational exchanges take place. Under the garb of such exchanges, the sleeper cells and terror viruses are being channelized into the system. Similarly, financial flows emanate under various obligations and are often backed by fraudulent financial practices including money laundering techniques. Besides this, educational, religious, cultural and economic ventures are also being placed under proxy control. Similarly, subversive tactics are adopted through congruent ventures abroad, where people of Indian origin are selectively nurtured to manipulate things at their home base.

It is also a matter of common awareness now that many frontal organizations and NGOs are used to act as 'agent covers' to modulate a 'war of perceptions', which is more fatal than a 'war of guns'. Given the awareness about the under currents and ulterior transactions, things may appear to be different than what they actually are. Various diplomatic moves, international fundings and public service projects are also under scanner. However, they cannot escape the eyes of public analysts who can see the different psychological operations that are targeted to control the local populace, in tune with the futuristic objectives of the global handlers.

It is under such a scenario that we must keep the 'terror profile' in mind while developing our response modules for various situations on a time scale. It is only a brief summary, but sufficiently indicative of the volatility of the situation. Added to it are the games of political allegations and counter allegations in a free democratic set up where various types of stratifications generate public biases, largely depending upon the 'hats' that they put on. The brutal realities are often lost in such situations where media generated perceptions confuse 'urgent' for the 'important' and vice-versa. The simmering trust deficit leads to distorted versions of terrorism and terror impact. The multiplier effect breeds terrorism. Thus, public perception, political response, bureaucratic decision making and operational handling may constitute a matrix where vectors may or may not conjoin to find an optimal solution.

Craft of Counter Insurgent Response

All wars end in peace. This is truer about internal conflict situations. The sooner peace prevails to allow the political process to begin; the better it is for the entire Nation. National security imperatives broadly determine the mode of interventions in handling insurgency situations. These include National policy, strategy and executive directives of the government. Whatever may be the modalities, the action of security forces in conflict zones must have a civil face and be purported to strengthen the civic authorities.

In the Indian condition, law and order is a state subject, while the Government of India through its Ministry of Home affairs coordinates the responses on the internal security grid. The Constitution provides for deployment of armed forces by the Central government to aid the civil authorities, subject to the given conditions and well defined modalities. Checks and balances have been created to dissuade unilateral discretionary decisions by the executive governments at any point of time, whether in the centre or at the state level. Operational powers to the forces deployed on counter insurgency grids are governed by the code of criminal procedures and special power acts for the specified forces in the areas declared as 'disturbed.'

The 'Group of Ministers' report submitted in the post Kargil situation recommended a comprehensive action plan towards reconfiguration, modernization, capacity building and healthy sustenance of the central and state forces, besides clearly bringing out the essentials of deployment modalities and the operational command for various situations. This also included specialized jobs for the central police forces and paramilitary segments. Standard Operating Procedures and a Unified Command System for synergetic results were also well spelt out to cater to multi-agency functioning in the operational area.

In fact, the local populace is the real centre of gravity. The tug of war between the terrorists and the state authorities hovers around this centre of gravity. Both would succeed on the basis of the support of the local population. Terror tactics may result in short term gains to those who are committing atrocities but cannot provide sustainability.

In any human mission, various ingredients of healthy management policies must find their way. Clarity of goals, consistency and congruency of purpose as well as effort, a high order of credibility of those who are leading the mission, transparency in performance and a common consensus on the targeted results are some of the key principles. These principles hold good in this tug of war as well.

The craft of counter insurgency response must be 'people centric' and should also provide them with an assurance of a secure environment. We must rightly assess the aspirations of the local populace in the conflict zone and chalk out all our strategies so that the implementation of our strategies results in winning the hearts of the people. It goes without saying that public perceptions are often based on mass communication domains. The past experiences may provide cognitive filters for interpretations. It has been empirically observed that there could be multiple silent communications emanating from the basic vectors of human synergy. Accordingly, the public information system and media management skills become powerful tools. However, actual performance and image building exercises both go hand in hand. None of these alone can fetch the desired results.

The actual performance would, inter alia, depend upon how the authorities handle the security as well as developmental concerns. Hence, the unified command concept under the chairmanship of the executive head of the state becomes important so that optimal assimilation of security and developmental concern take place on its own. Secondly, core groups for various purposes may be formed under a unified command to periodically coordinate the operational aspects in real time with utmost synergy. We may use any of the terms to define such agencies whether in the form of line or staff functionaries, overt or covert agencies, back office or the front line operators, so on and so forth. In functional terms it could mean planning, financial, developmental, police, armed force, intelligence and other auxiliary agencies.

In order to properly mould the environment, the balance between attrition and adaptability has to be fine tuned as we mature on the conflict grid. Attrition could be indispensable in an initial crisis situation, like a surgeon operating on the human body under conditions of criticality. Nevertheless, the surgical operations must gradually result in an improved homeostatic condition of the system, leading to a complete take over by the normal practices. Various civic action programmes are designed to cope with the situation during the period of transition. One has to reconfigure the plans which may congruently link security and development domains.

In fact, a think tank may be formed with a wide representation, ranging from multidisciplinary experts to the local people, capable of providing a feedback on the hard realities as well the pulse of the populace. They could, in fact, be the catalysts of change, besides being reliable couriers of information. We may remind ourselves that we don't only have to manage the geographical terrain and the physical infrastructure, but also the human terrain with the help of various soft skills. This calls for dynamic leadership.

One thing, which is crucial under this game, is the covert psychological operations. The handling of clandestine support groups and manoeuvering of the under currents form the core of such secret operations. Secret tasks though kept a secret are nevertheless both, crucial and critical. So, the lesser said, the better.

Managing stratified human terrains with vast vested interests may not be as simple as it appears. Hence, a proper blending of tactfulness and appropriate diplomacy could be one of the unavoidable choices in the larger public interest.

Till the desired equilibriums are attained, which would always remain sub optimal at different levels of conflict, appropriate circles of isolation as well as confluence are built to sanitise the existing domains and manage the 'spill over' effects. We may start with 'lose-lose ' situation and then move through 'win-lose' options in order to finally culminate with a 'win-win' outcome. It is imperative to perpetually underline a holistic approach and achieve progressive integration.

Besides the inherent typicalities of conflict management within the 'circles of hate', we can also have an 'approach-approach' conflict amidst the authorities handling conflict at different levels. At times, one may differ just for the sake of differing. At times, there may be a hidden agenda or one-upmanship issues. There could even be a difference of control dynamics at the union or federal level. The deficit of trust between various control centres may result in response deficits and 'escape avoidance' tactics for passing on the buck. It makes one wonder where the buck starts and where does it stop. Such situations are dangerous. Hence, a larger consensus may be required to keep the deviations within controllable limits.

CHAPTER II

OPERATIONAL DYNAMICS

"All things are difficult before they are easy".

—Thomas Fuller

Operational dynamics encompass the core domain of security forces, may it be the local police or the armed police forces of the state or the central paramilitary forces, deployed to aid the civil authorities.

Geographical Terrain Mapping (GTM)

(i) Traditionally, the lessons in 'operational response modules' commence with the repetitive focus on GTM and combat formations appropriate for the given terrains. GTM is still the basic foundation on which any operational design is built. However, now it has taken the form of a customized Geographical Information System (GIS). GIS modules provide for multi layering of geographical and operational data in integrative formats for better decision support systems. This also includes simulated modulations to cater to all the plausible contingencies. Various battle planning suites are available with microscopic precision for configuring 'combat assault' options. Core GIS is also supplemented by real time satellite images to assimilate the visual changes, locate the footprints of the adversaries and launch pin pointed offensives. This may be made more user friendly through PDA (Personal Digital Assistance) equipments provided to the fighting troops on the ground, granting appropriate connectivity for two way transfer of data. GPS guided devices are used for GTM and real time tracking, on the spot upgradation and data assimilation. Thus, GTM techniques have also advanced from paper maps and the compass to customized digital GIS.

Human Terrain Mapping (HTM)

(ii) Operational managers on the combat grid soon realized that GTM data bank is not enough. Ground situations demand proper HTM for the purpose of real success and stable sustenance. The operations, therefore, have to be people centric, depicting a humane face. Winning minds and hearts is not only essential for creating good intelligence sources, but also to keep public support on the right side and dissuade them from being influenced by the adversaries. In this tug of war between security forces and the insurgents, the swing is determined by the public support. Hence, it is imperative to know the local populace, their demographic traits, socio-cultural ethos and prevalent stratifications. In other words, it is essential to decipher the human terrain in terms of local ethos, pathos and logos on the basis of which the public support swings. Perception managers and handlers of public support groups, the social elite who can change the course of events, and last, but not the least, the link pins who become the catalysts of change forms the critical vectors of any HTM matrix. A systematic database with proper correlated inferences needs to be embedded in our decision support system (DSS).

Table - 1
Human Terrain Mapping (HTM)
It helps to : • understand who is not an enemy. • develop cultural intelligence. • establish multifaceted socio-cultural interface in the region for meaningful intervention and stabilization. • understand behavioural dynamics of the local populace. • determine need for various experts and resource persons as advisor to the commanders in handling. local ethos or forming cogent teams. • locate the vectors relevant for political security.
HTM does not purport to know who the enemy is. It focuses on who is not the enemy. It saves you from local alienation and shows ways to assimilate.

Terrorist Profile Development (TPD)

(iii) Terrorist profile development and the modus operandi analysis (MOA) are the domains which need to be scanned regularly. The more we know about the adversary, the better it would be to reap an operational advantage. TPD would include each and everything we ought to know about our target group. It ranges from identity data to his capability and capacity indices, it encompasses his modus operandi, funding channels and networking domains. Modus operandi may differ from group to group and place to place. Jehadi groups have been using car bombs, human bombs, 4-5 digit remote control mechanisms and lately the mobile triggered mechanisms for explosions. Maoists have been found to be using wired detonation devices, claymore mines and pressure bombs clubbed with well chalked out ambush strategies. Northeast insurgents have used ambush tactics at sharp hilly curves, making direct attack from a height and then using traditional weapons and implements to wipe out the disabled soldiers. Over a period of time, they have also made use of various explosive devices. Extremists on all the grids have freely used women and children as couriers. Indoctrinated youths have been used as front liners. Hence, it pays to conduct a strength, weakness, opportunity and threat (SWOT) analysis of the target group so that one can predict their possible moves and plan proactive operations with an inbuilt defence. It also helps to know their support system in terms of Open Ground Workers (OGW), besides the frontal organizations who take up their cause in the game of 'perception manipulation'. TPD, MOA & SWOT would help the security set up to plan for their own capacity building and organizational development.

Grid Deployment

(iv) Grid deployment is generally recommended for any professional force to effectively manage the conflict zones, more particularly when there are multiple forces. Manageable geographical grids are planned along with standard ground rules. Specialized security forces or outside armed units are brought in to assist the local civic authorities. Hence, a joint consultation mechanism needs to be put into place. There is a very commonly narrated tale of a crippled person taking the help of a blind. Both functioned successfully together by taking advantage of each other's positives. This is one of the best anecdotes on mutual synergy and it says it all. Hence, it is advisable to get the AOR (Area of Responsibility) or the operational grid in mutual consultation and draw out the overall plan. However, within the AOR, for the purpose of launching operations, professional decision should be taken by a specialist force in view of the intelligence (vision) provided by the local police. Under the GoM directives, the standard operating procedures have been suitably devised. The phrases 'in aid of civil authorities' and 'professional response within AOR' need to be underlined and well understood to avoid any ambiguity or heart burn. Such situations may lead to silent miscommunications and dominant conflicts within the official circles. This gives an opportunity to the adversary to reap the advantage and reconsolidate. There cannot be anything more immature than this.

The concept of grid deployment can also be used to configure functional domains in order to facilitate well targetted 'operational offensives'. In fact, with increasing reliance on specialised operational units, the functional domains are generally taking precedence over the geographical demarcations. However, the point of synergetic coordination amongst various units on operational grids remains the focal area. The line of difference between 'win-win' and 'lose-lose' situations often remains thin. The grid dynamics has to be understood with a holistic approach.

Table - 2
Deployment of Central Forces **Ingredients of Standard Operating Procedure** • Deployment of central forces in aid of the federal states on submission of a proper proposal/request • Assessment of operational need and congruent intelligence feedback • Preparation of operational plan through joint consultation mechanism and determination of grids/area of responsibility (AOR) • Professional autonomy to central forces within the AOR, conduct of operations either jointly or with the help of local representative of the state/civil police or independently • Use of police powers in specifically designated area, granted through special power enactments • Provision for local logistical support and operational intelligence • Joint periodical audit of performance • Review of deployments

Intelligence

(v) Intelligence is another critical vector on the counter insurgency matrix. Nothing much can be achieved by the forces without proper intelligence. Rather, they would be subjecting themselves to avoidable risks. 'All dressed up with nowhere to go' situation can be mitigated by getting specific operational intelligence. Intelligence inputs may range from public driven information based on trust and support developed by the security forces; human intelligence through dedicated and targeted sources, called "assets"; analytical intelligence based on the trend analysis as well as co-relational depictions; and the technical intelligence gathered through surveillance on electronic gadgets and cyber communication used by the adversaries. Out of all the alternatives, 'human intelligence' calls for careful handling. The game of nurturing the proper sources and using them optimally is not everybody's cup of tea. It calls for precise selection, development and care through tactful transactional processes, including quality 'strokes'. One also has to guard against the possibility of double crossing. Series of validations and cross checking may be needed. Advanced options also include planting the agents, improvising the "assets" and introducing them as useful resource persons in different work situations. It may also mean prompting subversion in the domain of the adversary i.e., developing a mole in his team. Various support groups may be developed and sustained under the garb of socio-cultural or humane missions. Psychological operations could also be leveraged through third party interface or intervention.

'Intelligence' exists in the environment in some form or the other, as nothing can happen without the local support. It is now essentially a game of wit to successfully capture it. Most of the time, it comes in bits and pieces and in coded formats, which may be difficult to decipher. Hence, constant and widely networked follow up may be required, where various observers correlate the trends in order to scan and filter the "truth".

CIR Dynamics

(vi) Dynamics of 'counter insurgency response (CIR)' on the part of the fighting troops or the police has to be understood with complete care and concern. In intensive conflict zones, every decision comes with a high possibility of error. Security is either hundred percent or zero. There cannot be anything in between. Similarly, success in CIR is either hundred percent or zero. In fact, it could even be drastically negative. Once we have looked into the essentials of CIR in terms of operational dynamics there should be no room left for any ambiguity.

Camp and establishment security:

(a) Camps and establishments of the forces in the conflict zones are easy targets. In J&K, tactics of grenade attack, car bombs, suicide squads, etc., have been used regularly. Naxals have also made attacks on camps in huge numbers, targeting them from well-secured domination points. In the northeast, one also finds examples of attack by rocket launchers. Hence, camp security drills have to be thorough and in place. There could be multi-layered security to make any access to the camp difficult, there could be well protected camp designs, there could be mobile parties outside the camp area, there could be ambush points in the approach route to the camp, so on and so forth. One can also make use of electronic surveillance systems, which may include CCTV, radars, imagers, magnetic or electric fields, auto barriers etc. Contingency drills should also be in place along with proper communication and force supplement options. Audit and reviews, along with rehearsals, are the much called for imperatives.

Area Domination

(b) As part of the area domination exercise, various actions are called for. Some of the basics could be –

- Understanding long and short run patrols
- Developing geographical familiarity
- Strengthening local contacts and rapport for information generation and support
- Identifying ambush & counter ambush points
- Planning operational movements with specific targets to ward off the infiltration in the area of responsibility.

In any of these exercises it is essential to keep in mind the following aspects:

- It should be purposeful and well planned.
- Necessary preparations be made in advance.
- Route selection, along with timing, mode of traversing and pace are critical.
- Element of surprise ought to be a priority.
- Nothing should be done as a routine.

A small case study would amply highlight the core concerns:

Case

The station house officer of one of the police stations in the areas affected by Maoist violence got a tip off that Naxalites have been looting material from the trucks on the National Highway at a place about 4–5 kms south west of the police station. The SHO sent a requisition to the commanding officer of the armed police force camping in that area. The young company commander, after due operational assessment, immediately responded and accompanied the SHO along with a one platoon strength. The SHO had with him two subordinate rank officers and more than sixty special police officers (the local people were selected to assist the police as special officers). The party left at about 10:00 hrs. and reached the given place at 1120 hrs. Reportedly, they found a newly built naxal camp that consisted of several hutments. It appeared that the naxals had left the camp and moved towards another hide out. It is learnt that security forces (SF) took their time to conduct a search of the camp. Whereas the SPOs collected a few items of their choice, the SF troopers burnt/destroyed the shelters. This provided sufficient time to the Naxals to collect their PLGA formations. On one hand, the SF troopers on getting the clue started marching towards the hideout; on the other hand, Naxals laid an ambush for them. Naxals threw certain items enroute to prompt the SFs to follow them in the given direction. They also planted minor IEDs to confirm the belief of the SFs that the enemy was not far off. The Naxals led them to a clear killing zone in the jungle where they had another camp. The camp bore the look of habitation and comfortable existence. This camp was about 13-14 km. further away from the first one. It was late afternoon by the time SF troopers reached this place. The allurement, the timing and the killing zone chosen by the Naxals left the SF troopers tired and in a hurry to go back. The SF troopers took some rest here before they headed back. The two platoons of PLGA with a well coordinated headquarter segment had already positioned themselves at a height and surrounded them in an infallible V-shaped ambush.

It is learnt that as an aftermath about 24 SF personnel had to lay down their lives. The naxal casualties are not known, though an informal feedback indicates an equal loss on the other side as well. The weapons of the killed SF personnel also fell into the hands of the Naxals. This case study highlights the following issues:

- The initiative taken by SF and the moves made by them
- The need for proper operational assessment and tactful advancements

- The overzealous action beyond justifiable limits
- The adversary's tactics to lure the SFs into a trap and drive them to the killing zone
- The combat skills of laying an ambush and counter ambush

Data Bank

(c) Constant up gradation of the data bank and real time flow of qualitative inputs is a must for purposeful and error free planning.

All wars are first won across the table. That is true about police operations too. Top leaders have to carefully strategize the operations. Blind orders or unplanned moves may result in avoidable heavy casualties. All the basic decision parameters ought to be considered thoroughly without wasting time. Even all possible contingencies should be provided for. The contingent chain of command should also be clearly defined.

Equipment Profile

(d) Appropriate equipment profile must be planned and provided for. This may encompass the following arenas:

- Security gadgets
- Means of mobility for different purposes
- Navigational tools
- Precision firing under varied circumstances
- Communication equipments
- Anti IED profile
- Survival aids
- Ready to use medical kits

Technological options are available in different formats and configurations to cater to various operational requirements. Hence, a right choice must be made lest one be misguided by the 'vendor driven' choices, which may not be compatible with the user requirements at a given point of time. Different security standards, varied compatibility options, wide ranging spectrums and usability imperatives call for due caution. Further, every technology needs soft skills for its application for which the necessary capacity building should be undertaken. There are instances where the best of equipments could not be put to use, as the troopers did not know how to use them. Smart systems, in integrated formats, are also available with intelligent processing and decision taking capabilities.

However, these technologies are available to the adversaries too. Moreover, every technology has a counter technology. One must, therefore, not forget that technologies are often self-subversive.

Technological options are often the force multipliers, though not always. When to use them and when not to, should always be predecided vis-a-vis the circumstances. Technologies also have a high obsolescence rate. Moreover, they involve exorbitant costs. The issues of their consistent use and timely upgradations are equally relevant. Lead organizations generally put such force multipliers into two categories, i.e., 'essentials' and 'desirables'.

Operational Tactics

(e) Operational tactics are of critical importance in the conflict zone. Surprise, deception, precision and perseverance are the essential components for success. Ambush and counter ambush plans must be well in place with a clear view about the degree of combat power to be used. As the tactics of direct confrontation have been replaced by guerilla like attacks and use of IEDs, the counter insurgency responses have to be proactively modified. Area intrusion tactics call for a proper review. Multiple intrusions in small teams, well networked for various contingencies have also been found successful in such situations. Single point intrusion in large numbers may result in heavy casualties, if ambushed by the adversaries in terrains with which they are more familiar.

Some of these issues clearly emanate from the following case study:

Case

During one of the winter months, at a police station 'Charlie', district Code N-111, the SHO received the information that a dead body was lying on the road near the village code 'Victor-78'. The police party along with an armed police contingent headed by an Asstt. Commandant left for the place. The parties were divided into two segments, one on foot and the other on motorcycles. It was a distance of about 16 kms to the spot near Victor-78, where the parties had to reach. The contingent on foot was further divided en-route into two sub groups. Thus, all the three groups were moving one after the other, maintaining a distance of about half a kilometer between them.

As learnt, the naxals, observing the pattern of their movement, laid down the IEDs in a fashion that simultaneous blasts forced the parties to take up positions just where they were. This resulted in not only physically separating them from each other but also preventing them from successfully reaching out to provide each other any help. As a shrewd move, the naxals had already smartly envisioned the places where the moving soldiers would naturally take cover on seeing the IED blasts going off around them. The naxals had already taken position at a distance covering such shelter points. Not visualizing the trap laid out by the adversaries, those who managed to escape the IED blast, tried to seek cover in the nearby trees and boulders in order to escape the sharpnels. But instead were hit from behind by the naxals who had already taken strategic positions. Thus, each of them was killed selectively.

Knowing well that reinforcements would follow; the other group of naxals had laid down landmines to dissuade the additional troops from trying to reach the place of incidence near the point 'Victor-78'.

About seven lives were lost along with a cache of automatic weapons of the security forces.

Here, the issues for ponderance could be:

- The analysis of the nature of information and cross verification
- Options to seek civic help in information of an investigative nature
- Appropriate decisions on composition, distancing, movement of the parties
- Area intrusion tactics, the scope of multiple entry and exit points
- Use of area weapons in jungle terrain for proper dominance

Area Intrusion Tactics

(f) Area intrusion tactics form the core of the operational plan. Adversary has the advantage of initial surprise attack if we permit him to do so by providing him with the opportunity. Experience shows that following tactics may mitigate the advantage to the opponent:

- Demarcate the core area
- Decide cross country navigational routes and movement drills
- Form small, compact, well equipped teams to operationalize the plans
- Evolve a multiple entry scheme with proper planning for timing, terrain and distance
- Formulate and codify the simulated offensives or change of movement keeping in view the various eventualities
- Use surprise and deception in what is being done
- Ensure proper halting and camping drills
- Place reliance on GTM, HTM and INT
- Plan for retreat and debriefing session
- Optimize command, control & coordination functions

Counter IED drills have to become a part of the daily agenda while moving in such areas. SOPs should accordingly be upgraded and modified to avoid any type of ambush. Effective camouflage of men and equipments including vehicles is also imperative:

- Update GTM and HTM data base of the area
- Form well equipped teams for advance search
- Define effective search procedures as per the terrain
- Follow deep observation techniques
- Adopt cordon-off and neutralization procedures on suspicion
- Decide damage minimizing movement tactics
- Keep place specific SOP in mind

Similarly, drills have been evolved to counter the designs of the adversary to attempt to perpetrate through sabotage, infiltration or subversion. Hence, essential security drills need to be followed as depicted ahead:

Essential Security Drills

(g) Major drills are depicted as follows:

I: Anti Sabotage Drills

- Assure nothing, believe no one and check everything
- Conduct systematic search, using all available means, covering inch by inch
- Use technical expertise to know IED configurations
- Cordon off the area and neutralize the suspected object
- Build-up data base

II: Counter Infiltration Drills

- Physical sealing of the area
- Coverage by surveillance equipments
- Using intercepting communication devices
- Seeking support of local populace
- Conducting well networked perpetual counter insurgency operations in the area

III: Anti Subversion Measures

- Keep data of all the human resources at work.
- Evolve infallible identification procedures.
- Enforce effective access control.
- Follow the need to be present and need to know principle.

- Evolve discrete checks and verification drills.
- Monitor unusual behavior & responses.

Major Ground Rules

(h) We are now in a position to summarize the major ground rules as follows:

- Cross country, self-innovative, GPS guided routes are anyways superior to using vehicles or walking on the beaten tracks.
- Avoid stereotyping, symmetry of time and activity. to mitigate predictability by adversaries.
- Discern the pattern of local activity.
- Look for tell-tale signs in the local environment and observe the locals for any mischief on their part.
- Generate deception in all of what you do to generate counter fear amongst the adversaries.
- Don't neglect but don't blindly trust either, even the best of human 'assets'.
- Document each new fact or pattern and analyze it.
- Conduct in the field has to be very alert as well as careful. All bad habits and routine responses have to be discarded emphatically.

Casual approach could prove to be fatal. Let us see a case in this regard.

Case:

In one of the cases, police received the intelligence that insurgents had put landmines around all such places like the abandoned forest guest houses, school buildings, panchayat ghar, etc., where the forces may temporarily seek shelter. On the basis of this information a party was sent to conduct a check. They confirmed the reports. The superintendent of police then sent more troopers along with Bomb detection and disposal squads (BDDS). The troopers had taken the local civilian vehicles. However, BDDS had carried mine proof vehicles (MPV). A part of the route that happened to be a common route for all civilians was covered by vehicles, while the rest was covered on foot. The expert teams diffused the circuits and recovered the IEDs from one of the schools. The team members were ecstatic as they had tasted success. The building contained all the maps and diagrams of the circuits.

Having successfully conducted the required search, the troopers rushed back. They followed the same route and then boarded the vehicles. Some of the staff chose to enter the MPV along with the BDDS team, thinking that it would be safer. The troopers followed tactical SOP till they were on foot but became relaxed once they had boarded the vehicles. Just a few kilometers before the camp, the MPV was tragically blown up in a powerful blast that had used a heavy amount of explosives. The vehicle was thrown up in the air by the impact of the blast and then it fell on the ground killing all the 12 people inside it, who probably died succumbing to a spinal/neck injury. Being excessive in numbers, they had not made use of the vehicle's safety belts which cost them their lives.

The issues for deliberation could be :

- Could the information be handled at a higher level?
- One could read between the lines, it was a ploy by insurgents.
- The troopers could have avoided the same route for return journey.
- There was no sense in having a convoy of mixed vehicle. Presence of MPV attracted the adversary's attention easily.

- Traveling in MPV in excessive numbers and without following safety norms was highly unprofessional.

Contingency Drills

(i) In fact, similar situations could be simulated in advance and brief rehearsals done. Such one minute rehearsals become invaluable when automatic responses are generated from the sub-conscious self in times of crisis. Thus, contingency drills should be specifically codified with due maneuverability for the commanders on the spot.

Jungle and Urban Warfare

(j) Jungle and urban warfare tactics are fairly different at times, subject to the physical terrain and the degree of colaterality. For instance, there could be a hostage situation in a crowded urban place like Mumbai or there could be an attack and a hostage situation in a town like Srinagar in Kashmir. Here, the configuration of civic structures would call for different tactics. The risk of collateral damages may vary. Hence even the urban warfare may have differential response patterns. Similarly, responses in jungle areas of Chattisgarh or Andhra Pradesh would be different. Thus, much depends upon the ingenuity of the commanders, though the basic essentials can be clearly spelt out.

In contrast to the case seen above, there is an example of tactful handling in a semi urban situation:

Case:

A specific intelligence was received about the presence of militants in Harwan area of Srinagar, J&K. Immediately an operation was planned by the security forces, forming various cordons to surround the area. The militants were, in the meanwhile, kept engaged with firing. The striking parties also occupied tactical positions during this period.

The cordons were slowly narrowed as the exact location of the militants was ascertained in the house of a local resident. Use of small arms and tear gas munitions did not succeed in forcing the militants to come out of the house. Grenades were launched which resulted in the upper storey of the house catching fire. It may be mentioned that the neighbouring houses were evacuated to avoid loss of life of the local residents. Enough precautions were taken to mitigate collateral damages. It called for tactful firing and proper coordination of all the teams. In order to avoid cross firing, the shooting was targeted at the ground floor where the militants were now known to be hiding. Having determined the position of the militants from their retaliatory firing, a couple of 'Heat rounds' were fired using CGRL. This accurate and precise firing destroyed the stronghold of the militants.

SFs then followed the room clearance techniques and recovered the bodies of two slain militants.

It appears to be a case of good planning, tactful handling and optimal use of weaponry.

We can now evolve basic rules for jungle and urban warfare.

Proactive Steps For Jungle Warfare

1. No deployment in the area for long durations.
2. Small team operations.
3. Use of Public Transport.
4. Live of the land. Be self sufficient.
5. Not to enter the village, not to take any help from the villagers.
6. Cross country navigation, no use of tracks and metal roads.
7. Planning and briefing of operation at higher level.

8. Maintain secrecy about operations & the movement.
9. Review the movement drills. Close monitoring of field movements.
10. Evolve proper halting and camping drills.
11. Debriefing and rectification of mistakes, training modifications
12. Proper reward and motivation.

Proactive Steps to Handle Terrorist Attacks in Urban Scenario

1. Proper policies and protocols.
2. Preventive security modules for all the important installations and places of public gathering.
3. Protocol for various security systems.
4. Digital mapping, videography and records of all the places of public visit/movement/halt.
5. Periodical familiarization by special forces/their rapid response units.
6. Regular training and equipping of special forces/ rapid response units.
7. Simulation, practice and audit of various tactical moves and operational drills to cater to attack, hostage, holocaust situations.
8. Proper evacuation, rescue and relief plans for all possible eventualities including usage of CBRN agents.
9. Networking with various agencies in town for an integrated response as required.
10. Synergy between various emergency services.

The use of IEDs with remote controls/timer devices/ mobile phone trigger mechanism on one hand and the potent combination of high and low grade explosives, easily available for commercial purposes, have accentuated the security hazards. These are low cost-high impact options. Two cases of U.P. are cited as small examples, though there has been a global upsurge in these trends.

Case-1:

An IED was placed in a Mahindra jeep and parked near Ram Janmbhumi, Ayodhya by a group of terrorists. One civilian was killed while another was injured when it exploded. The terrorists were gunned down by security forces while trying to enter inside the temple. The explosion had extensively damaged the iron fencing of the protected area. Post blast investigation revealed that a remote control mechanism was used to detonate the RDX based explosive.

Case-2:

An IED exploded in a general compartment of the Delhi bound Shramjivi express, damaging 3 coaches, killing 9-10 passengers and injuring over 60 others. IED was reportedly placed in a bag under the seat of a compartment. Some timer device was used to trigger the same, as could be gathered from the analysis by various agencies. ANFO, the nitrate based explosive mixed with oil, was used in a loose ratio.

The use of car bombs has been common

Case:

A Maruti-800 car with IED was placed near a school in Sonwar, Srinagar, J & K. The car bomb was meant to target an army convoy. One Army Gypsy was eventually targeted. It resulted in the loss of 03 army personnel and 01 civilian, while injuring more than a dozen other personnel/civilians. Post blast investigation revealed that it was an RCIED, using electronic detonators. Damage indicated the use of high explosives in the mixture along with low explosives, made of sulphur/aluminium/chlorates, etc.

Human bombs have also been used the world over

Case:

A glaring Indian incident is the Rajiv Gandhi assassination case where a lady, fitted with explosives and detonation mechanism on her person, gained entry in the form of a media person and approached the targeted VIP.

People Friendly OPS

(k) One must believe in conducting people friendly operations and avoid civilian casualties or collateral damages. A humane angle and a supportive conduct pays in the long run. In other words, alienation of the local population may cause more problems if the local support swings to the advantage of adversaries. It would be highly unprofessional to allow it to happen.

Professionalism, therefore, demands that to the extent possible, situations of collateral damages should be avoided while unavoidable damages should be duly compensated for. Due provisions should be made in security related expenditure schemes for the purpose.

Damage Control

(l) Damage control drills should also be put in place in coordination with the development agencies, local support groups and the media. A transparent and fair approach always pays. There should not be any hesitation in accepting a mistake that is made during an operation which has caused undue harm to the public and rectifying measures should be taken right from expressing regret to taking all possible administrative and financial recourse.

Auxiliary Force Multipliers

(m) Auxiliary force-multipliers in the form of Special Police Officers (SPOs) and Village Defence Societies (VDS) are also useful, if used tactfully. Whereas they provide avenues of public interface on one hand, they also act as an effective courier of operational information from the public. The locals also collaborate with the security forces to conduct local operations and act as guides, watchers and spotters.

Surrender and Rehabilitation

(n) Surrender and rehabilitation policies are also a positive step towards confidence building measures and getting the disgruntled elements back into the main stream. There could always be some dubious, illusive or contemptuous surrender, but that should not be a reason to abandon the positive steps which may provide a platform for reconciliation. Rehabilitation processes are also very tricky. There may of course be many irritants as well. However, such moves showcase the humane side of the authorities and deserve due consideration. Operationally, surrenders can also provide useful inputs to neutralize the terror networks. Much depends upon how successfully we handle the situation to our advantage.

Investigative Trails

(o) Merely conducting overt operations is not enough. Investigative trails should be developed with respect to various aspects:

- Source of recruitment
- Source of training
- Source of arms and ammunition
- Details of group members
- Leadership profile and networking domains
- OGW support system

- Chain of supplies
- Shelter points and hide outs, dumping points
- Sources of funds, parking funds

Hence, interrogating the arrested persons, a thorough search of their places and hide outs, scanning people as well as the places for various documents, communication surveillance and analysis of the various inputs form the essential ingredients of the investigation process.

Interrogation itself is an art. It is a specialized job that calls for a multidisciplinary approach.

Sharp inter-personal skills, psycho-behavioural strokes, and cognitive manipulations with congruent communication techniques form the wide spectrum of this job. The approach should be to prompt the person to divulge the truth without any filtration or distortion. An adept interrogator is equipped with all the information about the subject and the related issues. He is capable of creating an environment where the person under interrogation will conducively unwind and interact without any emotional instability, fear, apathy or disinclination. He should also, in the process, be able to read the mind of the 'suspect'.

The process of interrogation is highly dynamic as well as flexible. There cannot be any set rules or tight brackets. One must look for cues in any form, whether one adopts direct probing tactics or takes the manipulative stance. Usual tactics are as under:

- Playing hot and cold, using variant conditions such as fear, hate, futility, isolation, hunger, sleep, love, ego, concern, self actualization, etc.
- Adopting 'You know that we know' approach.
- Resorting to patient and repetitive listening.
- Convincing 'I am a friend' - a faith arousal technique.
- 'Lie- detection' tests and physiological-pattern study.

In fact, all the responses of the suspect, whether they are physical, physiological or psychological, need to be observed minutely. These responses may be explicit, implicit or indicative. It is a mental game where one has to negotiate the terrain with the skills to corner the person for a show down.

Search, seizure and arrest are the legal actions and hence knowledge of basic steps would be desirable.

Table - 3
Search and Seizure **Minimum Procedures** • Cordon off the area and place security checks. • Unless operationally emergent, procure search warrant. • Seek creditable witnesses as far as possible from local habitat, if need be the female residents. • Women and children in the search area be isolated to the extent feasible. • Search party to undergo check before witnesses to avoid allegations of implanting. • Anti sabotage checks, room-intervention drills and standard search procedures be followed. • Look for various clues, material imprints, documents as per the input. • Seize the objectionable material. • Make an inventory list before witnesses and give a copy to the owner under his signature. • Document each step taken under search along with reasons for the same. • Handover the objects and documents to next competent authority at the earliest. • Avoid collateral damages and follow humane approach unless otherwise unavoidable.

Successful prosecution and conviction is the next desirable step receiving due priority. This has its own perceptional effect on society, besides getting the guilty to the book.

One of the surest ways to substantively neutralize a terror network is to choke the funding conduits or seize the parked funds. Various enforcement departments should, therefore, make synergetic efforts in this direction. It may be useful to glance through the sources of terror funding:

Table - 4

Known Sources for Terror Funding

- Voluntary contributions from support groups.
- Compulsory donations.
- Money from patrons including enemy states.
- Extortions.
- Stock markets, gambling, event fixing.
- Narcotics and psychotropic substances.
- Networking with criminal syndicates and gangsters.
- Counterfeit currencies.
- Sale of arms, ammunitions & explosives.
- Misuse of Banking channels.
- Legitimate/illegitimate business interests/ enterprises.

Civic Action Programmes

(p) Civic action programs (CAPs) have a multipronged effect. Where they act as confidence building tools on one hand, they are also tantamount to filling up the developmental gaps which may exist due to some security threats or otherwise. Such gaps may become the cause of disgruntlement, and shift the centre of gravity more towards the domain of the adversaries. Civic action programs ought to be based on local needs, ethos and pathos. CAPs, to the extent possible, should be organized on a participatory basis at the level of the community. Following CAP activities have been popular:

1. Community Welfare projects.
2. Youth mobilization projects including educational, cultural, sports, tourism related programmes.
3. Women empowerment projects in socio-economic field; domestic facilitation.
4. Cultural and entertainment activities.
5. Emergent public services; public utilities.
6. Programmes related to media and mass communication.
7. Vocational capacity building programmes.
8. Occupational assistance programmes/projects.
9. Preventive and corrective health projects.
10. Infrastructural small projects.

Public Information Portals

(q) Public information requirements ought to be treated as a priority in order to feed the correct version of the happenings as well as to neutralize various possibilities of rumour mongering or distorted reporting. Today, the visual/electronic media has a wider coverage. Partial release of facts or delayed versions generate adverse silent communications. Taking advantage of the power of mass communication, manipulation of public perceptions has given rise to a new tug of war. Under this, the war of perceptions has proved to be more potent than the war of guns. Under the perception management doctrines, various support groups are nurtured. Selected NGOs are put in front to carry certain activities which may generate unbiased opinions in favour of the establishment. Related to it are a series of psychological operations carried through third party interventions.

Agents are activated under cover and a fine confluence of favourable activities and public propagation is achieved to generate the desired perceptions.

Table - 5
Perception Management
• Have an open-ended interface with the media through media friendly formats. • Identify public support groups for opinion making and seek proactive responses. • Showcase the good performance through effective means, including celebrity endorsement, events/ shows, visit to work place, etc. • Participation in the social cause and earning goodwill as a humane organization. • Improve performance as per public aspirations, professional parameters.

Operational Refinement through Case Studies

(r) One of the operational essentials is to conduct a case study of all the happenings – favourable or unfavourable to ascertain the intrinsics of the performance of the troops. They need to be codified along with suitable modifications to the SOP, as may be deemed appropriate. In case we observe a lack of operational habits, on the job training/ briefing/debriefing could be organized. It must be a priority concern area for the commanders. On the job training provides conducive conditions for generating the desired learning. It can be further simulated for tougher situations. In fact, a habit formation should be practiced through a 'one minute rehearsal' before taking any step. It could save the troopers from taking a 'blind leap'. The best 'on the job training' can be generated from case studies conducted on the enemy. We can, thus, step into his shoes and be a devil's advocate to recheck the efficacy of our own plans :

- Can the enemy predict our movements?
- Can he lay ambush on our route?
- Is he laying trap or inciting us?
- Are we rushing blindly on any information or happening?
- Is the source information reliable?
- Are we entering IED prone area?
- Are we prepared against multiple flank attacks?
- Are we being observed, misdirected by locals?

In order to substantiate how operational refinements and learning can be effectively brought out, a few case studies are cited:

Case Studies

Case-1:

In an important town about 50 kms away from the district headquarters of a district in LWE affected areas which is also close to 'Abhujmad', is a popularly known inaccessible hide out of Naxals that has existed for years. Here the village huts are thinly spread out. Owing to the sensitivity in this area, one of the camps of the civil police and other security forces also existed in the town. Camps of the armed forces were also positioned at vantage points on the local security grid covering a patch of 10-15 kms Despite a close grid, the main camp in the town was attacked by the naxals. The main fighting group could not have been more than 70-80, but the remaining attackers that came from nearby villages were numbering about 400-500. This was learnt later from various sources. The camp had morchas on all four sides and an LMG post on the top which was probably manned by Special Police Officers, and the localites inducted to assist the security forces. It is believed that the naxals first won over the SPOs and then neutralized the morchas made for the safety of the camp. They also destroyed the communication network. Then it was not very difficult to attack the sleeping cops. The camp had no fencing. Rather, the tall trees surrounding the camp provided a convenient advantage to the attacker of remaining well hidden. It was also alleged by the local people and the press that a couple of cops and SPOs were found to be in an inebriated condition. This was owing to the liquor and the rich food that they had consumed during the course of the evening.

All said and done, the camp occupants were ruthlessly butchered. The naxals also planted land mines in the camp and also under the dead bodies before leaving the camp. Not just that they also walked away with all the camp weapons, explosives and ammunition that they could lay their hands upon.

The published details of the incident left the concerned officials wondering...

- Was the camp security not properly planned?
- Were regular trained personnel not deployed to man the security posts?

- Was there no information system in place? Movement of 400-500 attackers could not have gone unnoticed. It could not have been so sudden.
- Why the thick tall trees were permitted to flourish around the camp which could provide cover to the attackers?
- Was the reliance on SPOs foolproof?
- Could the cops develop a code of conduct for strict adherence in such areas?
- Was the camp security not assisted by the patrolling or area domination parties outside the camp within a given potential zone?

Case-2:

One of the most maoist violence infested area is the patch between location 'Delta' and 'Tango'. The district administration and police forces had good coordination which resulted in a series of operational achievements. The sub-divisional police officer at Tango had an effective information network. He received an anonymous letter disclosing the presence of a huge amount of money, looted by the naxals, at the village 'Xanadu'. The SDPO also got it confirmed through his 'source' that had been earlier instrumental in other recoveries of arms and explosives. Relying on the 'source', an operation was planned on October, 7th by the local police and the armed forces present in the area. The informer was also instructed to accompany them. The operation was planned for early morning the next day. The informer did not turn up at the given time. However, the commanding officers decided to go ahead taking the local guides along. The absence of the informer did not bother them. The initial route was traversed by vehicles and then the raiding parties abandoned the vehicles a few kilometers before the targeted destination. The destination was on a hill top which they covered in an hour's time. On reaching the hill top, the party found an abandoned hut. A search of the hut revealed the presence of a money chest bearing a tag 'Ninety five lakhs of rupees to be delivered to the Zonal Commander at Delta'. The Chest was sealed using a small ordinary lock.

In the zeal of recovery, they brought out the chest and assembled around it, pondering on how to open it. It was probably not considered how and why a chest was left abandoned with an ordinary lock and a chit disclosing the contents of the chest. Not following the laid down drills, one of the personnel picked up a stone and broke open the lock. As soon as the lid of the chest was lifted, a huge explosion took place. The rest is history. As learnt later, a few of them died on the spot while a few lost their limbs in that mishap.

- The incident throws light on the following issues:
- Cross checking the integrity of informers, analyzing the risk of their double crossing.
- Not undermining the wit of the adversaries and the traps that can be laid by them.
- Need for observing the obvious and following SOPs even if things appear too simple.

Case-3:

In one of the north eastern states, two sections of security forces were returning from their assigned tasks along with the civilian parties. They had formed a convoy of a total of six vehicles in which the first and the sixth vehicles were occupied by SFs as the front and the rear escorts. The road that they were following was unmettled and slushy. Here the convoy was ambushed by the insurgent cadres. The last vehicle specially came under heavy fire. However the troopers in the vehicle effectively retaliated. But, due to the heavy firing, the vehicle caught fire and exploded. Five people died and one was left grievously injured. The personnel in the front escort vehicle jumped out and took position. However, they could not accurately assess what exactly had happened. In fact, what had actually happened was that the convoy had been ambushed on a sharp turn. After the first five vehicles had crossed, they had targeted the sixth one thus making it impossible for the rest to realize what had happened. Since all vehicles maintained a gap between themselves, there was bound to be some distance inter-se the first and the last. Now the insurgents on the hillock fired from the top successfully targeting the rest.

The reinforcements reached very late. The insurgents had already planted certain ambushes in the likely directions from where the additional forces could possibly come. Owing to heavy firing, the frontal escort members too dithered away, some of them being injured while some were lost in the unknown territory.

The points to ponder could be:

- Was the convoy properly formed?
- Was there no need for road opening parties or area domination squads?
- Were the contingency schemes not properly drawn out?
- Was there a failure of command?

Case-4:

In the hilly/forested terrain of Assam, a search operation was launched. The troopers covered a distance of about 18 kms on foot while vehicles had been sent to the other end to facilitate their return journey. Two parties were formed to look for the insurgents reportedly hiding in the valley area. Six other parties were deputed to act as stop parties as well as the striking force on the likely escape routes. Two parties were asked to position themselves at strategic points from where an overall watch could be maintained. The departure and reassembling timings were also set.

The operation 'Hunt' was over in a few hours but the insurgents were not found. The troopers took another route where the vehicles were to wait for them. They sat in six vehicles forming a convoy. The commander chose to sit in the first vehicle. It had become a little late and the sun was about to set. The vehicles in the front moved faster, expecting others to follow them. The rear convoy, consisting of heavy vehicles, could not catch up with the fast moving front convoy which was made up of light vehicles.

Suddenly, quite close to the camp, the rear three vehicles were ambushed on a sharp curve. The insurgents had hidden themselves in the grass on the top of a cliff. The place was so close to the camp that even the road opening parties (ROP) did not bother to clear it, nor did any one else maintain an alert as they were mentally relaxed that they had almost reached the camp.

The troop lost nine members and an equal number of them were grievously injured. The insurgents fled from the spot before any further contingents could rush from the camp to extend any help.

The issues for consideration are:

- Was the operation properly planned?
- Was the configuration and the handling of the convoy proper?
- Was the timing and the place of attack chosen by insurgents 'a smart move' on their part or does it show undue laxity on the part of the troops?

Case-5:

Two militants attacked the Head Quarters of the security forces camping at Zakura in Sri Nagar, J & K. The militants made an entry into the camp through a side wall, resorting to fire on the front sentries. One of these militants was immediately neutralized by the rear sentry. However, the other managed to escape in the dense undergrowth. The QRT immediately came into action and reported to the Commanding Officer who chalked out a plan. Looking into varied possibilities, the security of the whole camp was strengthened as per the crisis management plan. A well coordinated attack was launched on the second militant. It was known by then through various intercepts and as a result of the examination of the dead militant that it was a fidayeen attack. Taking all due precautions, grenades were launched on the second militant hiding in the adjacent jungle patch. As a result of this, he started running towards the boundary, firing on the camp indiscriminately. The well positioned QRT responded and sprayed bullets, silencing him forever.

This forms a good case study of a multilayered camp security, division of task, well coordinated action and command excellence. In fact the whole operation ended within 45 minutes. There have been cases of fidayeen attacks where the laxity of sentries has resulted in the sneaking of fidayeens into the camps and taking tactical shelter. The panic reaction of the Jawans adds to the crisis. Such situations have often resulted in heavy casualties and prolonged counter reactions.

Case Study on Modus Operandi of Naxals: Main Outcome

It would be interesting to know the modus operandi of naxals. Results from one such case study are presented below:

A: Camp Security Drill

- Proper recce of area

- Establishing self defensive sentry posts and mines on access routes
- Proper communication between Section Commanders and the Head Quarter
- Observing any stranger or suspicious movement near the camp

B: Intelligence

- Intelligence units in all towns and cities
- Focal areas
- The places visited by police
- Strengths. and weaknesses of police parties
- Co-ordination between Police parties
- Source of information to police
- Techniques adopted by police

C: Tactics During Movement

- Movement in small groups
- Reorganizing near target
- Cross country routes
- Hideouts in jungle
- Night movement
- Messenger system
- Silence during movements
- Precautions during move

D: Offensive Drills

- Invite police in the traps
- Use well formulated Dalams for multiple ambush, direct firing, blast, looting etc.
- Clarity on arc of firing

- Concealment and camouflage
- Special password, code/signals or use of headband/ shoulder band/wristband of various colours for identification

E: Survival Tactics

- Focus on local herbs and vegetables
- Accustomed to animal meat
- Focus on medicinal plants
- Water harvesting
- Makeshift shelter

F: Important Do's

- Abide by the discipline
- Give back whatever seized
- Talk politely
- Pay proper price for whatever purchased
- Return whatever borrowed
- Pay money for the damaged articles
- Appoint sentries and look for covers on reaching a den
- Protect the weapons like they were one's own life
- Confine to the assigned task

G: Important Dont's

- Do not act on will
- Do not scold or beat people
- Do not damage the property
- Do not misbehave with the people
- Do not ill treat the prisoners or humiliate them

Case Studies on Terrorism: Trend Analysis

Trends emerging out of case studies on terrorism are also an eye opener.

- Involvement of educated youth, including engineers in terrorist activities. Majority of those arrested did not show evidence of being products of radicalization.
- A conscious decision by outside terror sponsors to go for Indianization/indigeneous formulation of terror groups to generate deniability options for them and to project the terrorist acts as a natural outcome of persecuting complexities and grievances.
- Shift to Improvised Explosive Devices fabricated out of dual use of chemicals, such as Ammonium Nitrate, Potassium Chlorate, etc.
- Selection of targets with a view to cause mass casualty and get widespread media coverage.
- Involvement of organized criminal gangs in acts of terrorism.
- Use of OGWs to spot talent for recruitment.
- Use of religious institutions to groom the required cadres.
- Frontal organizations tasked for spotting talent among the youths to be inducted into terror network.
- Recycling of terrorists/surrendrees
- Adopting communication practices to elude police agencies and escape from being intercepted.
- Use of well placed, elite people as OGWs .

Future Trends In Terror War

- Information warfare and cyber terrorism
- Use of radio frequencies for various types of infiltration, sabotage, subversion and attacks
- Surveillance through geopositioning systems
- Precision targeting from remote locations

Beat the Enemy at His Own Game

(s) It is essential to know your enemy well and what can be better than to beat him at his own game? A small success story, built as a case study, says it all:

Case:

The district Mike-1 is situated in the southern part of Central India which falls under the declared CRZ. The district is highly sensitive from the point of view of Maoist violence, so much so that it has witnessed more than a 100 attacks in the past 8-9 years.

A weekly market is organized at MV-79, a place about 70 km. from the district head quarters of Mike-1. The place is frequented by naxals and is highly IED prone. On one of the days, a platoon of security forces reached the market place during an area domination exercise. The platoon was divided into three parties of one section each, moving at a safe distance from each other but at the same time connected through radio network. One of the groups of naxalites, moving in plain clothes, attacked the platoon incharge who succumbed to his injuries on the spot. Simultaneous attacks were observed on other parties too, who retaliated with their weapons forcing the naxalites to take random shelter. Meanwhile, the information was passed on to the company headquarters to send reinforcements. The QRT immediately came to their rescue. The naxals then retreated and started fleeing one by one in a given direction. The composite party of the security forces followed in hot pursuit. The fleeing naxals then divided themselves into two groups forcing the SF contingent too to make two teams in order to chase them in the different directions where they were headed. As destined, a direct one to one encounter took place between the respective naxals and the SFs. Two naxals were killed and four arms recovered. The SF also lost one personnel and a weapon.

Here, quick communication, coordination, knowledge of the terrain and quick mobility paid dividends to the SFs. However, one could have had better tactical advantage if the standard operating procedures for entering the market place had been strictly adhered to earlier.

Stress Management

(t) Stress management and gauging of internal health is another core area. We are dealing with human beings and not robots. The human software is organic in character and very delicate. Hence, we need to address two issues:

- Are the troops facing stress beyond tolerable limits?
- Is their morale high?

Two case studies depict the frustrated response of the soldiers, deployed for long periods on the counter insurgency grids, far removed from their families:

Case-1:

In one of the central police forces, a constable posted near the Nepal border, shot down his immediate senior and a few others who tried to intervene or even attempted to come to his rescue. Initially, the reason for this violent outburst was attributed to his regular drinking habits. However, close enquiries revealed that the deceased commander had actually been taunting him on grounds of his belonging to a family of questionable repute, quoting the example of his sister having eloped with a muslim boy. The delinquent constable could not bear this constant humiliation in front of his peer group.

The case highlights certain core issues. The foremost is that the personnel of such armed forces who have to stay away from their kith and kin, regard their camp as their home and haven and look forward to a nurturing response by the troop commanders as well as their peer group. Further, every person thrives on his self-esteem which should not be hurt or lowered.

Case-2:

One of the constables belonging to UP and posted in Srinagar, J&K shot himself down. There was no apparent reason for this act on his part. The senior officers tried to brush it aside as it being a result of some personal issue. However, the sector commander did not buy this explanation and ordered a probe. The probe led to a series of revelations. The deceased constable had bought a piece of land after borrowing money from his father. He had sent an installment of Rs.15,000/- to his wife to return to his father as the money was needed immediately for the treatment of his mother. The wife, however, refused to hand over the money. As a result the deceased and his wife had had a series of altercations on the phone, just the night before. This fact was known to the PCO constable, the friends of the deceased in the camp and even the section commander. The episode leads us to various issues:

- Was there any mechanism in place to counsel the men on their family concerns?
- Did the peer group fail to provide due support?
- Was it not possible to grant him temporary advance of a meager sum of Rs. 15,000?
- Did he not feel free enough to contact his immediate seniors?

Table - 6

Findings Of Various Case Studies On Stress Management

	Stress Related Relevant Factors	Possible Solution Domains	Stress Management Formats
1.	Supervisory/ peer behavior	Individual sensitization	• Coping techniques • Self management training • Behavioural and leadership training
2.	Degree of conduciveness of work environment	Managerial/ leadership development	• Open communication • Work related welfare • Interactive activities • Healthy inter personal relations • Generating dignity for self • Respect for team members • Effective grievance redressal • Group cohesiveness • Command credibility, fair play & transparency • Motivational leadership • In house counseling • Healthy regimentation
3.	Level of internalization at individual level	Systemic aspects	• Career growth optimization • Empowerment in work situation • Continuity of command • Work load rationalization • Conducive working and living conditions • Family welfare • Risk compensation & rehabilitation policies

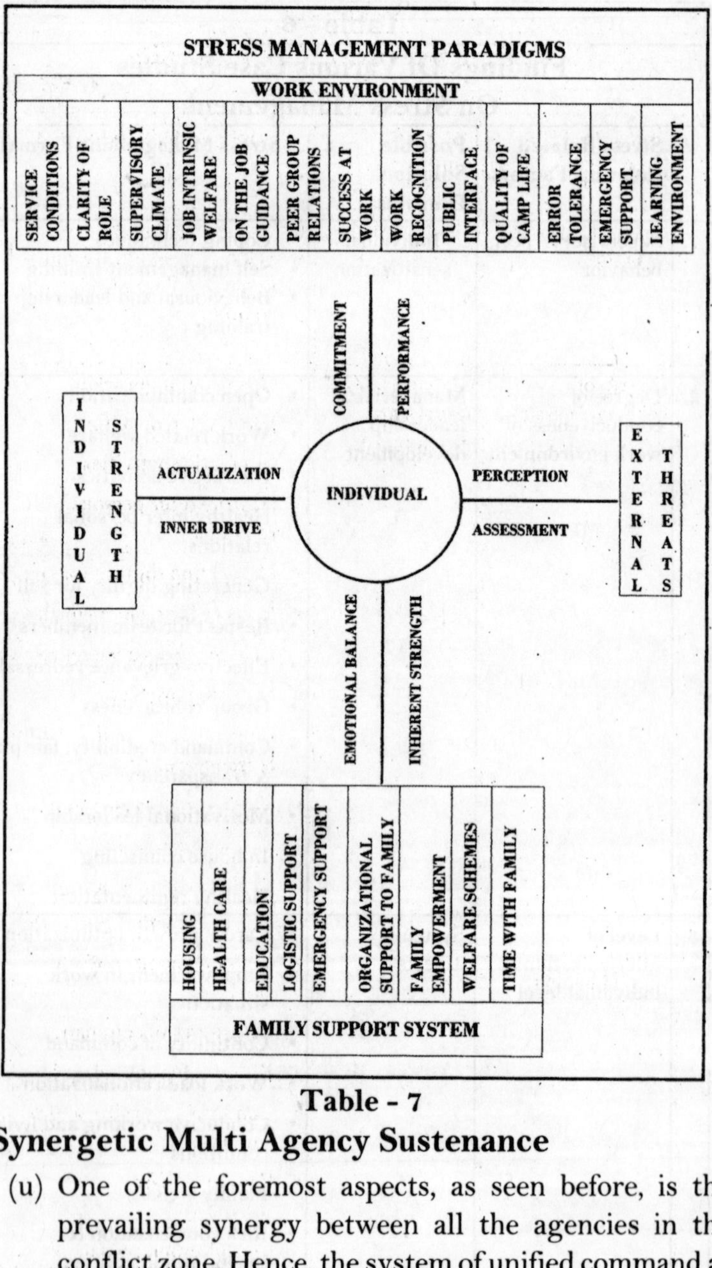

Table - 7

Synergetic Multi Agency Sustenance

(u) One of the foremost aspects, as seen before, is the prevailing synergy between all the agencies in the conflict zone. Hence, the system of unified command at the apex level and core groups at the operational level is introduced to facilitate formal and informal interface, as well as functional cordiality. There has to be a complete understanding of ground rules for cooperation between multiple troops. 'Real-time' exchange of operational information between intelligence agencies and the fighting troops is another core area. Any laxity would result in having to pay a very high price by all. At times, forces suffer due to losing opportunities to neutralize the adversary. 'Sources' take advantage of the rifts or undue suspicion between the agencies and gainfully play one against the other and exploit the situation. Despite ample awareness on these aspects, commanders refuse to learn their lessons. One of the quickest and reliable method, therefore, is that the commanders of the forces ensure that they have broken ice with each other and enjoy a healthy feeling of mutual respect and confidence. This demonstration effect shall automatically percolate down. Synergy transmits effectively to the cutting edge level through a proper demonstration effect.

Response Capacity Deficit

(v) At this juncture we may glance through the basics of analytical risk management for the operational forces. Risk here does not, and should not, mean risk to life or the quantum of threat from the adversary. That is a part of the job. Actual risk to security forces would mean 'Response Capability Deficit (RCD)'. This could be the deficit on account of critical factors. Some of them are:

- Lack of intelligence mechanism for timely operational inputs.
- Lack of proper strength and operational preparedness.

- Lack of proper logistics and operational inventories.
- Lack of operational powers and autonomy at the cutting edge level.
- Jurisdictional conflicts.
- Lack of clear command and operative guidelines.
- Lack of stress redressal mechanism.
- Lack of motivation and morale.
- Low tolerance level.

Local Adaptability Problems

(w) The Central forces deployed in federal jurisdiction may have diverse problems of local adaptability in the given environment.

Response Capability Deficit of Central Forces

- Role Conflict
  - Intrinsically a specialist force
  - Extrinsically in aid of the state
- Functional limitations
  - Lack of clear AOR.
  - Scattered deployments
  - Inadequate local response
  - Lack of local data bank
  - Lack of policing powers
- Deployment intricacies
  - Prolonged deployment
  - Lack of soft slots
  - Diversion of training companies

Operational Dynamics

- Lack of operational flexibility
- Inadequate managerial response
  - Goal displacement
  - Lack of operational leadership
  - Ineffective interpersonal relations
  - Poor coordination & networking

CHAPTER III

THE THIRD EYE

"You cannot depend on your eyes when your imagination is out of focus".

—Mark Twain

A Deep Vision

In a low intensity war situation, we tend to lose out if we come to a stand still. And if we make a move, that has to be intelligent enough to derive the best possible advantage over the adversary. A smart course of action, therefore, calls for a timely operational input translated into a winning situation through error-free implementation. Hence, what we need is the 'third eye', a deep vision which would scan through all the essentials:

- all plausible inputs regarding strength, weakness, movements and missions of the adversary.

- all plausible information on the geographical and human terrain in the operational grid.
- all 'must-know' details, in terms of capabilities as well as response capacity deficits, with respect to the operational team members.
- all likely contingencies, analytical outcomes, in the given environment, taking into consideration the past incidents and the future extrapolations.
- all the requisites for a synergetic output.

2. Thus the real intelligence for a commander is to acquire a holistic view of all such vectors on the operational grid which may otherwise put him to a disadvantage. He must believe that his adversary is doing nothing which is accidental. There is no point in merely chasing the trail of a tiger.

3. The fundamental aspects, as above, often find mention in the expositions of various experienced commanders. Some of them are:

- Carefully outwit your opponent in thought, design and proactive responses.
- Find the advantageous ways of waging the offensives.
- To optimize operational potentials 'know your enemy' and 'know yourself' well, that is, as holistically as possible.
- Study the plausible situation variants.
- Know when to fight and when not to. The opportunity to defeat is provided by the enemy himself.
- Know the people better than a mother knows her child.
- Familiarize yourself with the land better than the localities.

Good intelligence systems cater to the data base for all such pre-requisites.

Soft Power Development

4. The dynamics of intelligence hovers around the growth of soft power. Intelligence requires focused diligence and not aimless slogging. Analysis at every stage is the soul of this process. Without the timely inputs, one may find oneself in the awkward position of being 'all dressed up with nowhere to go'. Hence, the art of intelligence is an indispensable segment of the operational craft. It is not merely confined to building contacts, creating sources and agents or generating technical intelligence through electronic surveillance. In fact, a comprehensive data base regarding the target groups, SWOT analysis of the opponent and ongoing plans of the opponent form the core structure. Geographical mapping, human terrain mapping, incidence mapping, movement mapping, etc., are the continuing exercises for co-relational inferences. These are verified intermittently through inter-agency exchanges, interrogation of the surrendered or arrested insurgents and the like. Investigative leads are also essential to trace the human linkages, supply chains, funding conduits and the OGW network of the adversary. Human intelligence, based on key factors like proper talent search, source and agent handling, relationship domains, etc., remain crucial throughout. Since the technology is self subversive, the smart opponent often creates a 'fire wall' to avoid getting captured through technical surveillance or interceptions. There are ways to generate deceptive mirror images or pseudo workstations. There are coding and decoding techniques making it difficult to decipher the captured encryptions. Hence, technical intelligence based on machine generated data may not be reliable beyond a point. Intelligence can also be generated during operational movements, such

as combing and search operations. Advanced intelligence techniques also include covert perception management exercises, psychological operations and nurturing of support groups. Under the banner of Community Action Programmes also, besides generating cordiality and goodwill with the local populace, talent search exercises can be performed. In fact, the dynamics of intelligence suggests a need for constant R&D in all the above fields. Last, but not the least, it is imperative that we develop a capacity to undertake counter intelligence operations and neutralize the agents of our adversary subverting our systems. Hence, guarding against infiltration, sabotage or subversion of our intelligence networks is equally important.

5. The criticality of intelligence mechanism mostly increases when the adversary makes a base amidst the local populace and undertakes proxy war by using indigenous soft powers and resources. At times, public protests are also engineered to dissuade official action against the terrorists or insurgents. Proxy war through manipulation of local vectors on the security grid poses new challenges.

Dynamics of Intelligence

6. Amidst this background, we may now glance through the basics of intelligence which enhance the vision of the 'third-eye' and work as force multipliers in the true sense. Can we truly hit the nail on the head?

(A) Like water one has to find the path of least resistance. Hence, it is essential to develop a data base to know the local geographical as well as the demographic profiles. Thus, 'human terrain mapping' becomes more relevant here. Given the inputs of the geographical terrain mapping, along with accurate inputs regarding the opponent, we can hope to really manage our responses as per the time proven rule:

"Emerge from the void, strike at vulnerable points, shun places that are well defended, attack in unexpected quarters".

Experience shows that being kind and nice to the local population enhances the chances of getting good leads from the public and also acquiring quality "sources".

(B) One has to look beyond the surface and capture the under-currents to draw an operational advantage in the true sense. This calls for great analytical and extrapolation skills. These will come only when one has a deep understanding of the operational vectors and sufficient experience. One really has to keep alternating one's thinking hats as per the 'standards of the opponent' and then shrewdly decipher his moves.

(C) It is sacrilegious to remain ignorant about the opponent, as the opportunity cost of any error or omission would be heavy and irretrievable. In this game of moves and counter moves, one is required to repeatedly make use of quality sources. A good source is really an "asset". So, commanders without 'sources' are just as handicapped as a person who is both blind and deaf would be. Such a person is bound to lose. It is not a simple task to develop a source who can be a tactful spy. Every source needs proper and careful handling. The complexity of the task would be evident from the following disclosures in this business of spying:

- Only those sources can survive who have keen intellect yet appear to be shabby, dull and foolish. The source must be comfortable performing all sorts of incongruous jobs yet possess a sense of proportion, courage and integrity. He must follow the 'mouth to ear' secrecy principle not sharing them with even his near and dear ones. His intentions and any vital information is to be carefully held within him.

- One has to be careful and very alert when dealing with the 'source'. A 'source' handler must know the difference between honesty and 'double crossing'. Generally, the 'source' can be located from amongst the aggrieved categories, such as those persons degraded by the opponent, superseded cadres, fickle minded workers, punished criminals and the like.
- Those trusted by the adversary and accustomed to the luxuries of life, can also be pliable to manipulations. Functionally viewed, sources could be categorized as those who work locally, those who intrude in the opponent's domain, those who have worked for the opponent earlier but were enticed away, those working openly for one cause but catering to certain ulterior motives through deceptive means and finally the hybrid opportunists.

In view of the extreme sensitivity of the business of spying, we may suitably theorize certain critical aspects of source management:

Step-1: Undertake environmental analysis to determine the information deficit so as to evolve the scope of work for the source.

Step-2: Intelligently decide the required capability and capacity level of the source.

Step-3: Design capacity building domains for the selected source as per the need.

Step-4: Evolve motivational and a manipulative package to keep the source activated.

Step-5: Conduct cost–benefit analysis to nurture or neutralise the souRCE.

Once a source is operational, it would be imperative to evaluate the quality of his inputs in terms of their relevance, reliability and potency. It would not be out of place to state that under optimal conditions 'one should be able to traverse through and conveniently scan the opponent's stronghold'. Sub optima, however, may occur owing to various tradeoffs or compromises, at any of the stages. Whereas capability and capacity deficits may surface in form of response time, habits, resourcefulness, risk bearing attitude or various sets of skills required for the job, the sub optima in the motivational domain could hover around his primary and secondary motives such as ideological beliefs, feelings of reprisal, hunger for money, desire for importance, avoidance of an uncouth outcome or any other ulterior transactions that he may covet for.

In the whole process, therefore, the following aspects remain crucial:

- Source selection and handling, where we have to first develop our own operational capabilities in order to select an outsourcing partner.
- Secrecy and security of the processes, where we ensure building viable systems.
- Risk management, where we prepare against the possibility of double crossing by our source or his foolish modus operandi.
- Intelligence management, where we ensure multi agency cross verification before developing complete reliance on the 'source' or the 'asset'.
- Cost–benefit analysis, to arrive at a decision to keep the 'asset' alive or to deactivate him.

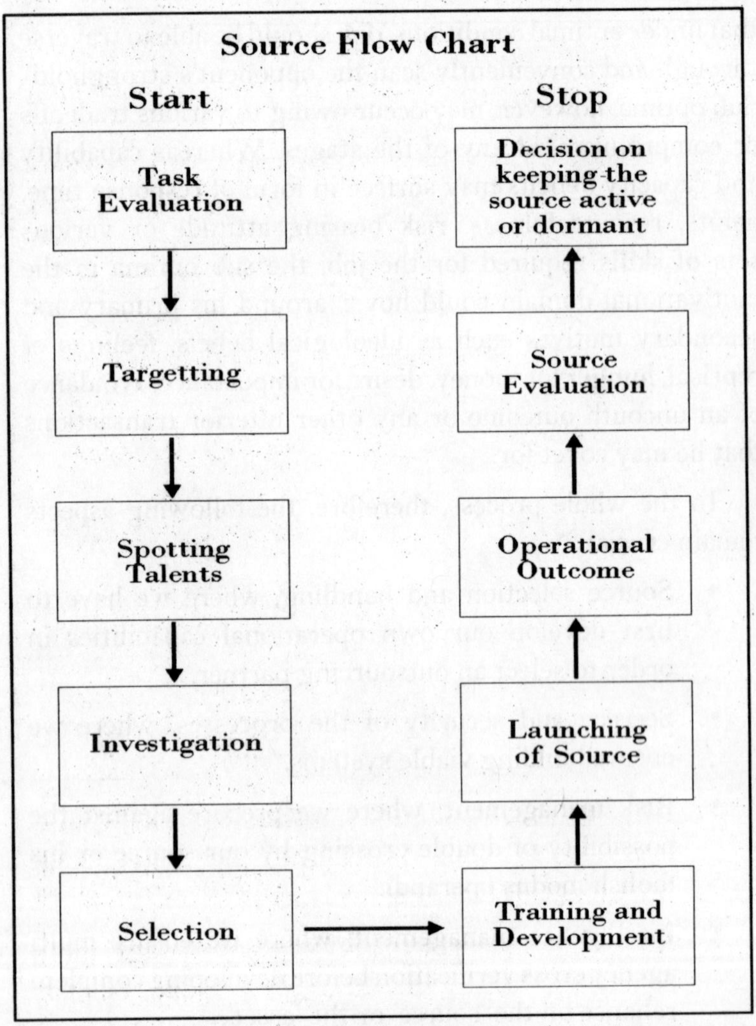

Table - 8

Where to look for a Source?

1. People running such ventures where they get the opportunity to openly observe various movements in the normal course (eating points, PCOs, religious places, grazers, small vendors of various types, hoteliers, etc.)

2. Unemployed youth
3. Disgruntled elements
4. Victims of the target group
5. Recycled members of target group/surrenderees
6. Refugees
7. Local marginalized segments
8. OGWs working for the target groups
9. Journalists
10. Local criminal networks – active as well as dormant.
11. Places of 'fun and recreation' that the target group can visit.
12. Students, educationists, professionals and experts
13. Local Govt./non Govt. functionaries in various capacities.
14. Retired cops/sleuths.
15. Advocates/Jail employees or service providers

Useful Tips for Running A Source:

- Observation (listen through eyes).
- Non linear thinking (evolving multiple choices).
- Attitudinal Leverage (free flow, yet controlled).
- Develop 'if-then' logic (extrapolate consequences of each move).
- Intimacy with the source (commitment towards the 'deal').
- Stepping into the shoes of the source (role playing).
- Evolve 'multi-fit' mindset (out of the box solutions).

- Evolving 'gambler's edge' (turning game to your advantage).
- Being offensive (proactive moves).
- Honour your skills and know your slots (confidence and clarity).
- Do not ignore analysis (know your history well).
- Train and develop the source (enhance 'usability' of the source).
- Do not get pushed aside (other players may dissuade you).
- Know when to get out (know 'risk limits').
- Never give up (be persistent).
- Direct control of the source (on the job monitoring).
- Tactfully manipulate the source (through his weakness/money/other motives).
- Beware of 'corrupt' practices of the source (he may double cross, use you for his gain).
- Keep source's interest alive (let him not lose interest in you).

(D) Clandestine operations are also within the domains of intelligent network purported to accomplish counter intelligence tasks, carry counter subversive or counter sabotage assignments and determine suitable measures to optimize such missions. High level intelligence operation can also be carried under different covers in order to hide its true nature. There may be "cross intelligence- transactions" in the process in terms of what we generally understand as double agents, working for both the sides but known only to one of them. This is a game of wit, patience and risk bearing capacity, as well as preparedness, as to how far one succeeds in penetrating the network of the opponent. 'Agents' or 'sources' may also remain dormant for a long period, to be activated in case of certain predefined conditions. This is suggestive of plausible variations in this game of intelligence and counter intelligence. The germs are released through such 'sleeper cells' which grow when activated. The movements could be very surreptitious, not leaving any foot prints. We may not go into the finer differences between what we call as 'contact', 'source' or 'agent' at this stage, which generally depend upon their nature and terms of deployment and long term dependability. One can sabotage our hardware, while the other can subvert our software. What extent of damage can an opponent do to us? We have to safeguard against such sneak attacks and at the same time play counter games. This is akin to the moves on a 'chess board'. Thus sabotage and counter sabotage, subversion and counter subversion tactics determine the outcome in the long run. A good commander does not give unnecessary importance to short term gains for the purpose of statistics. He optimizes the gains in the long run. Hence, make only stable moves, unless any contingency makes it imperative otherwise. There is no doubt that a successful operational commander has to be an expert 'intelligence-navigator'.

(E) Surveillance, a planned observation process should be used as discreetly and clandestinely as possible, with due follow up as it is one of the most effective ways of getting relevant inputs. We can use shadowing techniques to serve our purpose. Selection of proper persons for this job, trained well to perform error-free operations needs due attention of those in the command positions. These are high risk options as any failure can lead to many avoidable exposures, besides enhancing the threat level where infrastructural setup and operational plans could be the prime target.

Human surveillance has no substitute in many situations. However, with expanding technologies electronic surveillance avenues are available. They are far more speedy and accurate. Technological options, clubbed with smart intelligent systems, have shown wonders. But the problem with technology is that it is self subversive. With target groups getting enhanced exposure, counter surveillance technologies can be exploited the other way round as well. They can even use various 'fire wall' options to fence them, thereby conveniently eluding the electronic scanners. Electronic sniffers introduced by opponents can crash the targeted systems. False mirror images and pseudo base stations have been used to create deceptions in order to misguide the security agencies. However, we may keep using such options as long as our adversary does not negate them. Technological obsolescence also makes such options very expensive, yet they are desirable in view of the 'mass destruction' tactics of terror modules. The issue of opportunity cost may be important. But one should not forget the loss of public confidence. The cognitive damage is intangibly huge. Keeping these realities in mind, we can suitably use the following options, as per the opportunity our adversary provides us on these grids:

- Communication intelligence on various frequency domains: HF/ VHF/ UHF/GSM/G3/G4/HEM etc.
- Cyber Intelligence: e-mail/Internet protocol/chat rooms, etc.
- Image Intelligence: Satellite Image/UAV image.
- Other Sources: audio/video/documental.

However, the issues of database generation, standard operating procedures and secrecy still remain critical areas for the command system. It has also been observed that these technologies have a long learning curve vis-a-vis the rate of their obsolescence. This makes it imperative to build well qualified and dedicated teams to assist the operational authorities.

(F) Going back to our basic hypotheses, we can easily recall that security forces as well as terror groups need public support to succeed and sustain. Hence, the issues of perception management and psychological warfare become far more pertinent. The 'war of perceptions' has assumed a greater potential in today's world than the 'war of guns'. Amidst various operational checks and balances, there has been a natural shift towards perception management. What does it mean?

- Observe the target group and determine people's profile.
- Determine cognitive or perceptional deficits and evolve the required "strokes".
- Design the subject matter as per the HTM and available communication options.
- Adopt the appropriate mass communication modules.
- Evolve covert collaborative formats whereby a different picture is presented with respect to the players of this war of perception. Chose the 'poster boys' carefully.

Various support groups and NGOs may be nurtured to sustain this drive. Subject to the requirements, the degree of 'covertness' can be manipulated to seek the desired responses. However, a holistic view has to be operationally taken, rather than the piecemeal administrative decisions. The net 'impact' is more important than the 'processes'.

Bureaucratization of operational responses, therefore, should be dissuaded at any cost.

(G) Abundant lead inputs are derived from the analysis of the foot prints the adversary leaves behind at the place of incident. Hence, every incident needs to be looked into thoroughly, to have a reality check on the earlier inputs received regarding the adversaries. The situations encountered with the opponent, on being subjected to corelational magnification, have the potential to reflect on the intrinsics of the likely future moves. Developed in the form of case studies, they also provide a true evaluation of our preparedness and the existing response deficits. Investigative leads culminate in analytical intelligence derivatives beyond any preponderance.

(H) Finally, therefore, from the operational intelligence point of view, we may zero down upon the following domains within which we need relevant inputs regarding the opponent:

- Strength, skills and their spread
- Infiltration, exfiltration and recruitment
- OGW support
- Covert support and networking
- Infrastructure and supply conduits
- Inventory profile
- Political patronage
- Public perception
- Modus operandi – sabotage and subversion – fatality index
- Funding avenues
- Strategic vision
- Command and commitment

Chapter IV

Capacity Building

"Even if you are on the right track, you will be run over if you just sit there".

—Will Rogers

Capacity Building, both at organizational as well as individual level, is a dynamic process. It is primarily aimed at strengthening the core competencies that lead to an excellence in operations and the final deliverables. In aggregate, the response capacity is the synergetic 'end-result' of the quality of the human resource, constant training and learning, logistical and technological force multipliers, community collaboration and last, but not the least, the level of commitment coupled with a progressive vision.

Focus on HRD

Structural reconfiguration of the organization, development of logistics and induction of technologies are the 'inorganic' areas which can be duly addressed with the help of experts. Well customized solutions are available. These menus may not be cost effective in the short run. However, it is not difficult to choose the best from a wide spectrum of workable options which may give a favourable cost-benefit ratio in the long run. Out of all the factors, the most sensitive and delicate is the 'organic' domain of human resource. The field of human resource development is, therefore, the backbone of any organization. A wanting human resource will not deliver despite the best organizational structure, logistics and technological support. On the contrary, an effective human resource is bound to produce quality results despite weak support systems. Creativity, commitment and innovativeness are the key factors in such a case.

Automatic Response Capability

Operationally, capacity building should mean 'creation of automatic response capability' to cater to the situational exigencies in a given environment. In other words, the relevance of any system is contingent upon its capacity to address the needs and aspirations of its stake holders on a sustained basis. Taking a holistic view, the aggregate end result would hover around the following domains:

- Quality of Human resource induction.
- Learnings generated through training.
- Sustained work culture and habits.
- Integration of technology and logistics as force multipliers.
- Organic work environment nurturing people at work.
- Aspiration fulfillment and reinforcements.
- Growth related neo-equilibriums.

The integrated system's approach to capacity building provides the key.

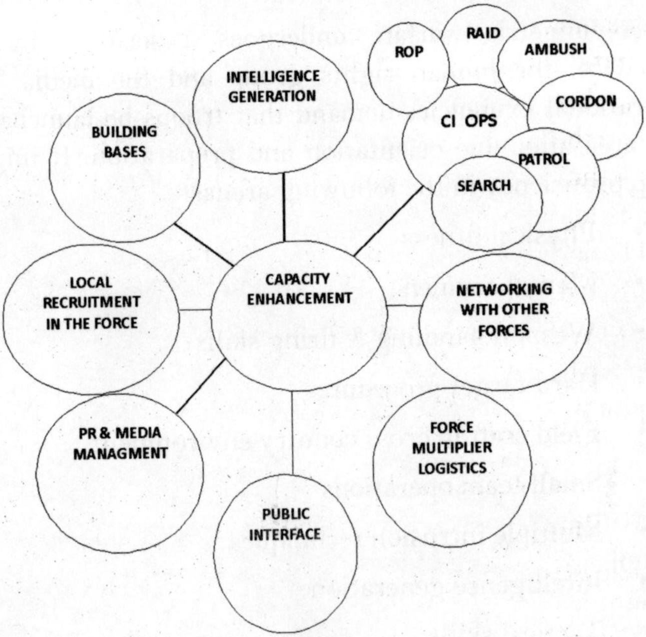

Chart - 3

Vector Calibration

However, there may be no linear solutions in low intensity conflict zones. Amidst various sub optima and professional irrationalities, viable conditions of stability have to be clearly located on the operational matrix. In fact, each similar situation may still be new, calling for a different set of 'vector-calibration'. High stress situations may easily lead to goal and role displacements, besides cognitive dissonance in the team. Negative entropy may be high, posing great challenges to the leadership. High error tolerance level may no longer remain an exception. Keeping in view all such centrifugal tendencies, emphasis must be placed on human resource training to optimize the homeostatic responses. Creating an automatic capacity to respond should be the litmus test for any such inbuilt human efficiency.

Asymmetric warfare undergoes a scrutiny by the populace, the human rights group and the media. The operational exigencies demand that troops be launched in the area after due orientation and preparation. It implies deep proficiency in the following arenas:

- Physical fitness
- Mental acumen
- Weapon handling & firing skills
- Hard target procedures
- Field craft in cross country environment
- Small team operations
- Multiple intrusion techniques
- Intelligence generation
- Tactical skills
- Use of technology at the cutting edge level
- Planning and coordination

Out of the Box Solutions

At the cost of repetition, it would be worthwhile to recall the basic parameters to be covered under the orientation process. There can be no two views that it pays to understand the genesis of the problem, study public perceptions, acquire a demographic and psychological essence of the ongoing conflict spectrum, and know about the key players and their profile. Whatever be the field exposure and the level of training, there is no denying that innovativeness and creativity are the key to operational success. One has to constantly evolve 'out of the box' solutions. Hence, an 'on the job learning by doing' is the ultimate answer. Understanding the concept of operations and the rules of engagement within the unbounded domains would always remain the core concern area for any commander, notwithstanding the complexities of a multi-agency environment.

Behavioral Sensitivity

Any exposition on training would not be complete unless we also merge the concepts of behavioral categorization of the people and the intricacies of human learning. Behaviorally, a person may belong to category 'X', when he is guided by the stick and the carrot policy; a person may belong to category 'Y', when he is self guided given a conducive environment and category 'Z' where one would suo motto effect the positive change, being at a high level of self actualization, howsoever adverse the environmental pressures may be. This has leadership implications with respect to the inner drives that need to be manipulated and suitably nurtured to arouse the desired responses. Different types of people may, therefore, need different 'strokes'.

Interestingly, the learning arousal in a given training environment may be subject to the following hypothesis:

- Maximum learning happens due to the demonstration effect by the role models or the peer-group.
- Putting the learners through a practical situation stimulates better responses which can be further modified through appropriate reinforcers.
- During the controlled learning situations, visual depictions have substantive and a long lasting impact, in comparison to audio inputs.
- A participatory approach has deeper impact than one way communication.
- More than content, it is the 'process' which we adopt in communication, that matters.

We need to pin down on the internal configuration of a person in terms of his perception, cognition and values which would guide his responses. A bad configuration would lead to destructive results despite the best technical learnings. Rather, a positive configuration may induce creativity and determination in a person to seek appropriate technical solutions even if the required skills are lacking in that person. Empirical cases often prove this preposition. Secondly, behavioral excellence is sine-quo-none for the police personnel as they don't build roads or buildings but deal with human beings, good or bad, and that also in crisis situations that require inter-personal cohesiveness. They are required to build bridges of mutual confidence. Perhaps, there is need to see beyond the superficial.

Emotional Stability

High risk jobs amidst difficult circumstances entail psycho-behavioral training so that the troops don't lose their emotional stability. Since low intensity war has to be fought in the civilian terrain where our own people are involved, utmost care has to be taken to locate the perpetrators who may strike at will, taking advantage of the initial element of surprise. Civilian casualties and collateral damages are to be avoided even at a risk to the troopers. At times, mass casualties may take place without any justifiable reason. Hence, in extreme circumstances of low intensity conflicts on the internal security grid, a high level of emotional stability becomes an essential condition for the troops to maintain their cool and show restraint. New offensives may have to be planned amidst unknown variants.

The stress capability level has to be high for other reasons too. Conflict ridden situations often call for their deployment in remote areas away from their family for long spells. Make shift living arrangements further reduce the minimum comfort levels perceived to be essential by the troopers. Thus, ways and means have to be devised to put them on a psychological flight. This may mean anything, right from ensuring conducive leadership drives, an amicable peer environment and self actualization to life style modulations amidst an adverse situation of scarcity.

This also brings to the fore the need for enhancing 'self management' capabilities of the troopers. Many of them could be a victim of self perceived frustrations and a lack of coping capabilities. The 'art of living' in such circumstances may be shared to widen their horizons.

Situation Specific Response

The variants in the operational situations are highly volatile such that each situation may appear to be new and unique. Hence, there is little scope for any preset drill to be applied on a text book pattern. It pays to simulate a situation specific response, hold a one minute rehearsal and then proceed. A Situation Specific Response (SSR) ought to be the guiding principle. It implies that there is no ready solution and there is no instant dose to recover from any operational problem. One has to be innovative as well as creative all the way. One has to generate an element of surprise and deception for the opponent each time. One has to strategically escape the enemies' ploy to lay an ambush in the process.

As propounded, any operational man without proper intelligence is like the 'blind and the deaf'. Hence, capacity building missions should focus upon a generation of analytical skills, the art of source creation and handling, use of technologically facilitated surveillance, etc., in addition to providing exposure to GTM and HTM modules. It may be reiterated here that any technology is self subversive. Its use has to be undertaken with utmost caution. When, where, how and how much are the basic questions that need to be addressed under each SSR.

The 'SSS' Principle

The experience in the highly sensitive grids shows that 'SSS' is the core navigational principle for the troops. This terminology, used by the paramilitary troopers as a generic connotation, stands for 'secrecy', 'security' and 'speed'. Secrecy of location, movement as well as the capacity to hit the opponent are all relevant here. Secrecy also implies strategies and counter strategies to generate, sustain and neutralize the deceptive moves. Timing is also of crucial importance. When one speaks of security, it refers to a guarantee of the proper equipping of the troops right from fire power to mobility, navigational aids, communication tools, protective gears, survival kits and medicinal first-aid options. Speed, as generally understood, could mean a proactive response, a fast 'on the spot' decision, and a briskness in physical mobility. Mobility would either provide an edge over the opponent or draw you beyond his killing zone even before he can react. Capacity building would, therefore, also mean the art of mastering 'SSS'.

Group Dynamics

Group dynamics is another such area which needs due attention during capacity building missions. It means –

- Proper selection of group members
- Due acceptance of leadership by the group
- Determination of mutual goals
- Evolving desired level of cohesiveness
- Designing communication and coordination modules
- Imbibing standard operating procedures for varied responses
- Agreeing upon conflict resolution norms

- Constantly striving to enhance the group synergy as well as the level of motivation.

The group dynamics is primarily contingent upon the operational environment, the configuration of the group, the leadership styles and a feed back on the group performance. However, the litmus test is that the group cohesiveness and chain of command should be able to withstand any type of situational pressure. The art of sustaining and nurturing high group cohesiveness may assume different shades, depending upon the framework we adopt. We may have formally structured groups, we may have loosely knit informal groups, we may have need-based partnerships or even open ended collaborations. Again, the modules so available could differ in their relevance quotient, depending upon the nature of the operational requirement. Since the situations are highly volatile, the finer combination of varied modules could be a better choice. It would imply that enough 'flexibility- windows' be provided while configuring a group. Thus, the adaptability level needs to remain high.

Whatever be the connotations or the domains of 'capacity building missions', the crux lies in the nature of the organic element, i.e., the human resource. Hence, any such exercise needs to be largely delved upon by the HRD. We must evaluate the HR deficits vis-a-vis the operational requirements and then focus on its proper development, including the integration of various force multipliers.

Crisis Management

Presuming that whatever has been visualized above is done to enhance the capability level, one issue still remains to be addressed. That is the arena of crisis management. The activities and sub-activities of various crisis situations must be duly visualized and identified. The response time too needs to be properly determined. The trigger points should be well listed. The mechanism should also be in place determining as to who will be the first responder and how the chain of response shall progress further. How the control room functions would be performed at the place of incidence, how they would be linked to various static points are some of the issues to be determined in advance.

It is important that 'Quick Reaction Teams' be part of every operational group. They should be well equipped. The mock drills and rehearsals could be carried by them through simulated modules.

Thus, capacity building in terms of human resource, equipments, training, intelligence, team work and appropriate responses in varied situations, with a given level of stability, forms the basis of success in any operational environment.

CHAPTER V

PORTALS OF PUBLIC INTERFACE AND PERCEPTION MANAGEMENT

"A successful person is one who can lay a firm foundation with the bricks that others throw at him".

—David Brinkley

Confidence Building Measures

Local populace or the community provides the basic foundation for any operational success. Those who enjoy the public confidence are the ones who can see through many eyes and hear through many ears. They are the ones who can have the synergy of manpower and the resources. In various conflict situations, the deficit of public confidence aggravates the tension levels and provides induced advantage to the adversaries. Like viruses, if the firewall is weak, they will make an entry and wreck the system. Decontamination may not be feasible beyond a point and the losses could be irretrievable. The dichotomies of public life have complex formats and it may not be easy to handle them with linear modules. The situation of social stratification and power groups, social elite could lead to oscillating sub-equilibriums that need to be understood for finer balancing. However, the flexible zones with common stakes are always available. Secondly, the masses can be addressed through various windows where the 'elite' may not be able to vitiate the moves. Hence, it pays to study the human terrain and know the cultural as well as behavioral response patterns. In fact, one has to locate the critical areas for assuming leadership through various means. Based on the study of public dilemmas and expectations at various levels, the partnership formats could be designed. Confidence building measures could be devised as per the local configurations. The extrinsics of the local configurations of a community setup could indicate an altogether different picture, sharply deflecting from the intrinsics, which is what really needs to be tackled. The public undercurrents again become important here. Silent communications need to be closely monitored. The demonstration effect of visual conduct and the 'spill over' of filtered information is what matters the most in mass communication. The perceptional filters, therefore, need to be underlined. Even if the administration, the operational forces adopt an open collaborative approach, the client relationship grids may not entertain the vectors which are otherwise regarded as highly acceptable. Public vision could be coloured by the vested interests through cognitive filters that they provide to the masses. Thus, the portals of public interface and perception management have to be understood and dealt with, under a wide spectrum of evident as well as hidden stakes. An open self concept towards the stakeholders is likely to pay dividends. The nity gritty of mass communication techniques, viability of civic action programmes, potency of community policing and victim rehabilitation schemes along with a nurturing response during crisis, may arouse public trust in the establishment. Amidst these centrifugal and centripetal forces, one has to provide the appropriate strokes to optimize the value of human transaction, for operational as well as the larger public gains.

Winning The Hearts And The Minds

Since people constitute the centre of gravity, winning the hearts and minds is crucial for an operational success. If we take various subsets, the position would emerge as follows:

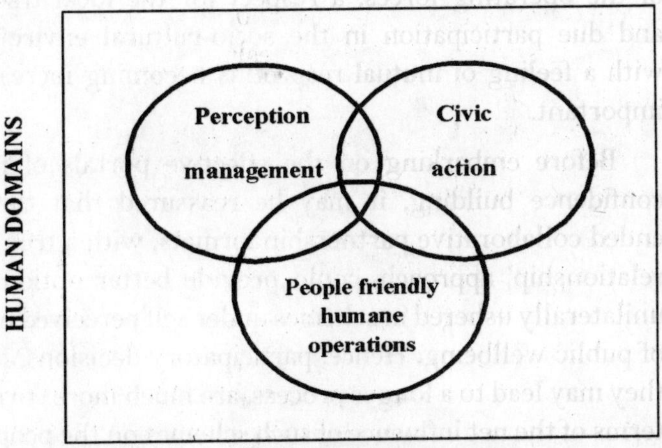

CONFLICT ZONE

Chart - 4

The highlighted area depicted by the mutual intersection of the three subsets needs to be expanded as a quotient of operational success. While adopting various modules under each subset, it is imperative to keep in mind the relevance as well as the acceptability of the measures being undertaken. Given the geographical and human terrain, along with the socio-cultural and historical peculiarities, every conflict finds its expression and relief outlet in a unique fashion. Hence, a plethora of vectors on the local matrix have to be duly correlated and optimized. Nothing much really can be done in isolation. The holistic entropy then becomes pertinent. The various efforts made in these directions can have a hard as well as a soft option. The concept of congruent software, an appropriate operating environment and compatible hardware, as applicable to the virtual world in cyber space, are more relevant in the real world. The techno-financial project evaluations cannot ignore the social-behavioral indices in the operating environment. This could also mean that the enhancement of infrastructure or logistics is just not enough. Factors such as the social behaviour of the operating forces, a respect for the local traditions and due participation in the socio-cultural environment, with a feeling of mutual respect, is becoming increasingly important.

Before embarking on the effective portals of mutual confidence building, it may be reassured that the open ended collaborative partnership formats, with a true 'client relationship' approach, could provide better options than unilaterally ushered in schemes under self perceived notions of public wellbeing. Hence, participatory decisions, though they may lead to a longer process, are much more coveted in terms of the net influence of such schemes on the people and their desired conditioning. Principles of social leadership, group dynamics and mass communication (not forgetting silent communications), thus, rule the roost.

It may not be so easy to seek public cooperation and the desired response in the high intensity zones as the fear factor, the terror impressions of the adversary may be far reaching. Any development initiative or humane operational plan first needs to be properly blended with an effective security cover in the area. So often, there are initial chances of such efforts going to waste. However, the confidence building measures should be designed and redesigned for an onward journey as there is no scope of retracing your footsteps. The centre of gravity should not be missed. Otherwise, there is a likely chance of falling into the vicious trap of the 'imbalances'.

Image Building

At this juncture it may be fruitful to glance through the basics of image building so that all the efforts made by operational agencies in the conflict zone don't miss out on the binding factors. The following excerpts are relevant.

"Image" is the strongest silent communicator. It reaches faster and much before a person or organization can even think of reaching a place. It colours the cognitions of the target group. Precisely, an image is a set of beliefs about an entity in the mind of others.

It is based on credibility, visibility and approachability. It is the ultimate perception, built upon performance and further multiplied through branding exercises. Each of us is consciously or unconsciously striving to be identified with the positive image of the organization we work in. Image building is crucial, as the net effectiveness and acceptability depends on the image we enjoy. It then nurtures our level of the overall bliss. Having agreed on the basic premise and its desirability, it is not difficult to learn the art of image building. However, before carrying forward our understanding on this much neglected, albeit most desirable art, let us have a brief look at the image building tactics being resorted to by the competitive entities in an open system.

It has now been realized by management theorists as well as its practitioners that an open and transparent interaction is essential for healthy and stable communication. Our acceptability would depend on how we can proactively judge the needs of others and respond favourably to fulfill those gaps. There has to be an appropriate shift of focus from the subjective to the objective, insider to the outsider and 'this side of the fence' to the 'other side of the fence'. That is how opinions, in their holistic format, tend to evoke a silent communication. Here the role of the media is crucial. The sensitivity increases manifold as they are in a position to transmit strong audio-visual data to generate 'information' for people which affects their cognitions. The experience with the media shows that we may, ceterus paribus, adopt following tactics for nurturing healthy relationship with them:

- Open networking
- Mutual recognition
- Proactive interaction
- Sharing information in the media friendly formats

The next important segment is society itself. One cannot survive nor progress in isolation. Social back up is essential. In fact, as an integral drive to give the necessary push to ones image-building, social groups become an elementary need. They can give the necessary boost. Supportive groups can play a vital role in the potential growth of one's image.

Genuine involvement in a worthwhile cause helps in leading to the proper 'spread' of the desired aura and popularity. Blessed with these characteristics one can make congruent use of one's abilities to discover, define and resolve social problems and related issues. Using ones positives, to convince and induct voluntary support for relevant issues from various places, can help to garner public interest and attention. Approaching public issues with an openness and interactive methodology ensures acceptability.

Being in a position of 'command and authority' one can convert this into a positive tool to mitigate nefarious activities, regaining more and more public approval and acceptance. Encouraging an open house policy, where ones activities and style of work are granted the appropriate recognition, gives one the necessary hype and adulation. Organizing common media events, that drive home the necessary points to reinforce ones efficiency in varied quarters, further encourages public acceptance. Introduction of schemes and policies that involve sustained public interest in ones organizational capacity tend to reduce problems, issues and conflicts through media propagation. Symbolic support from a celebrity or an important public figure further provides the necessary endorsement and weightage to the organization. The following strategies, thus, become crucial for image building:

- Identifying public groups for networking like associations, clubs and other similar bodies.
- Evolving community support groups like peace committees/voluntary help groups, etc., for wide open collaborations in order to achieve common missions.
- Identifying problems and adopting proactive steps for their mitigation.
- Sponsoring public activities.
- Inviting people to visit production centres/places of work and exhibiting professional excellence for client oriented delivery.
- Organising events, shows, seeking public indulgence.
- Introducing promotional schemes for branding organizational image.

- Getting an endorsement through some VIP or celebrity.

It is essential here to understand the basic parameters governing positive communication. Positive communication starts with a trust which comes, intrinsically, from the role one is expected to play and the sincerity with which one performs it. It is further flavoured by the 'moods and emotions'. One can also change the cognitive and perceptional background of the people which forms the referral base for interpretation. Thus, both, the content and the context, are important. Since people don't have direct access to all the data and information, they rely on the 'authentic channel or couriers'.

Consequently, the ways and means of communication also become equally important. Primary ways are better than secondary, though the former may have limited coverage and is also constrained by time and cost factors. The value additions in image building are also subject to the holistic and the synergetic currents when viewed in a compact format. Thus, essentials of effective mass communication are to be well understood before one can appreciate the importance of the tools.

To continue with the main discussion, one can also focus on what is generally called as 'social cause marketing' i.e., identifying common social problems like health, general welfare, education, child-care, women-empowerment, etc., that become viable zones for concerted intervention. Public acceptance on such burning issues is a very strong image enhancer. Humane projections, endeavouring to bring to limelight the social issues that have long remained dormant and much ignored, evoke positive public response and sympathy. Thus, we have more options with us –

- Identifying social issues relating to health, education, children and women empowerment.
- Initiating collaborative social projects for problem-solution.
- Earning goodwill as a humane organization.

Regular enhancement of image through realistic and genuine strategies, geared to indicate a well laid move to produce the desired levels of credibility, is a must. Carrying on visibility and credibility enhancement exercises from time to time as an inseparable part of mass communication strategies, keeping in view the intrinsic ethos of the local community, are of crucial import in this arena. Meaningful interaction has to be initiated as a planned move. The formats may then depend on the creativity level of the organization, given the behavioural response of 'clients' and 'stakeholders'.

The two basic premises are to be well understood by us in order to imbibe the true art of image building. Firstly, 'Good Performance' is inevitable i.e. quality of work output is an essential condition for a good image but that is not enough. We may have to still resort to brand imaging exercises and activities to channelize public sentiments in our favour. Secondly, a good branding exercise alone may sharply enhance our image but would fall in geometric progression if it is not consistently backed by a good performance. Thus, both are complementary as well as supplementary to each other.

One need not be bogged down by the intricate expression of the above premises. They might appear obvious but should not be taken lightly. As we relive them again and again, they would eventually invoke the innumerable layers of our ignorance. One needs not only to be good, but appear to be good as well. We often forget how to 'appear' to be good.

This is not something which we think others should view us as, but infact, what actually others would view. Hence, our concern should be to study the 'other-side' and the communication processes influencing the cognitions and views of that side.

Configuration of the receiving end and the reception intricacies assume greater significance at times, unless the sender is strong enough to mould the environment to his advantage. We should, therefore accept these premises on a serious note and not a lighter vein.

The performance oriented credibility factor is nicely explained by a statement which may sound simple but is extremely relevant, 'what you speak is so loud that I cannot hear what you say'. We need not go into the extrinsics to prove our point. A little focused attention or observation to our surrounding environment would help us to realize the intrinsics as well. The interpretations, after all, follow from the image, i.e., the credibility of a person. As goes the famous saying, "What is said is not important, who says it is more important". Now we can draw our own lessons.

Coming to the Police Organization, it is essential to realize what people want in a good police. The brand image exercise, as true for the open competitive world, is fully relevant here too. Gaps in the service delivery system can be bridged if one adopts and imbibes the client-relationship approach responsively. Clients, stakeholders are to be well recognized and given due importance-structurally as well as behaviourally. Clients may vary from public to democratically elected 'controlling-elite' and from our seniors to the juniors.

Collaborations, networking, open exchange, shared information, empowered roles and flat structures are the success-rules to gain maximum 'performance-synergies'. But police often presents a contrast. Various security agencies are often seen working at cross purposes or making ulterior moves in order to keep the individual scores high.

Image building has to be a part of the work culture and the onus lies on every link-pin in the ladder. Handing over this task merely to the PRO does not and cannot work. Even a onetime extravaganza of community action programmes alone cannot lead us to a win-win situation.

Such exercises should be inbuilt in every action that the police takes. It is a public service, but cops live under the false perception of superiority, coupled with self-claimed secrecy. They work in isolation keeping the real stake holders at bay. They shun criticism, hence denying the avenues of growth. They remain in a world of their own fallacies and make-believe surroundings, as the colonial legacy and bureaucratic culture still enslaves them.

Civic Action Programmes

Civic action programmes (CAP) are effective tools not only to address the problems of developmental deficits but also to establish strong public interface and provide a congruent response to the public sensibilities. They provide an operational edge to the security forces, as a higher confluence of cognitive consonance is achieved. This not only facilitates effective communication during crisis but also the flow of useful operational inputs. Well planned CAPs don't limit themselves to a one time or short term disposition but focus on the long term sustainable projects.

The different programmes under such schemes could be summarized below for the sake of clarity and sample listing:

- Youth welfare programmes focused on tapping their energy towards constructive avenues and dissuading any diversion by disintegrative forces. It may include the arenas of sports, educational tours, professional training, employment and career counseling.
- Women empowerment projects aiming at domestic consolidation and life style enhancement, augmentation of generic skills to undertake economic projects, development of avenues in the field of art and culture, literacy programmes and domestic health care as well as nutritional nurturing.
- Community level collaborative projects in the field of social integration, economic output, professional facilitation and cultural consolidation.
- Health care projects including emergency response systems.
- Public work projects to facilitate augmentation of civic amenities.
- Projects related to environmental protection.
- Special area specific projects, such as micro power plants, solar energy, rain water harvesting, etc.

The 'CAP' provides windows to address the situation of hostile psychological reactions by the local populace amidst ideological counter propaganda by the adversaries. Thus, the gap of perceptions and festering mistrust could be mitigated to some extent. Although the situations are fraught with grave implications, the redeeming feature is the inherent commonality of purpose that is to establish normalcy and allow socio-economic activities to take place.

The most important aspect is to identify the opportunities of intervention and appropriately configure the mode of ushering in the CAP initiatives. Following aspects need to be studied carefully for proper appreciation:

- Causes and effects of alienation drives by adversaries.
- Cumulative effect of the cultural differences enhancing propensities of mutual conflicts.
- Economic stratification and divide, marking the faultlines for exploitation.
- Misunderstandings emerging due to the failure of communication between the people and the police administrative system.

'CAP' Domains

The key innovative domains need to be evolved to neutralize the above anti forces and find the right course for reconsolidation. Some such domains could be:

(1) **Reaching out:** Reaching out to the people by whatever means ought to be the core strategy. One of the shortest method is to approach them through the community elite and the media, as they control the perceptions of local populace. Till the ice is broken between the security forces operating in the area and the community, they can prove to be strong mediators. Gradually, the attempts can be made to develop a direct rapport and win the local trust. One can also reach out through the electronic media and radio services via interactive programmes. ' Phone-in' facilities can be integrated during such programmes for real time responses.

(2) **Benevolent Interaction:** In the background of the long drawn economic and social hardships, besides the

emotional ruptures, lending of a helping hand could arouse a good response, if done in a concerted manner. Adoption of villages for growth, empowerment of youth, promotion of local culture and sports, health and hygiene projects, resettlement projects for the widows and orphans of militancy are some of the windows to enter the hearts and minds of people and depict nurturing benevolence.

(3) **Culturally non-intrusive:** In all such programmes, it needs to be consciously kept in mind that there should not be any imposition of the outside culture. Programmes ought to be in consonance and conformity with the local culture and the ethos. The intervention, preferably, could be discreet and understated.

(4) **Respect and Humility:** It is important that a position of superiority is displayed nowhere in dealing with the people. Even in economic interventions, care has to be taken to project utmost respect for those who receive the aid. Aim should be to evolve partnership rather than domination. Troopers should be sensitized to follow a humble approach. The message which should filter in is that security forces are there to help the people to get back on their feet and reclaim their rightful lives, rather than become dependent on external forces.

(5) **Partnership in the Mission:** It is important that the mission gets strengthened through a more robust public partnership, right from the planning stage. Care is to be taken to see that people evolve along with the maturity of the projects so that their lives become self sustainable in the due course of time.

(6) **Constant and Understated:** The effectiveness of the project can only be ensured through its continuity and commitment. One time random interventions are better forgotten as it results in a lot of negative

feelings because it raises the hope and then leaves them with unfulfilled deficit. Propaganda and moralizing attempts should be totally avoided. The message has to be subtitled, understated and should be pegging on the effectiveness of 'silent communication'.

(7) **Progressive:** The project sponsored ideas and concepts ought to be progressive, integrative and developmental. In many projects, the inclusion of target groups such as children, the disadvantaged social lot and remotely settled populace devoid of any modern day development, as the beneficiary group, often pay rich dividends in terms of goodwill generation and public cooperation.

Such programmes have a far reaching impact in terms of acceptance and reducing hostility. Contiguous areas too have a spillover effect and provide avenues for further linkages. Human interaction, when it is multi-dimensional and a two way process, tends to become complex. However, such efforts add meaning to local life styles in terms of new encryptions and a creation of neo sub-texts.

Victim Reassurance

Victim reassurance programmes should also be integrated with CAP, even though such programmes fall more in the domain of the administrative setup. However, owing to indirect denial of access to developmental agencies in the area due to security threats, such schemes may better be intertwined with the civic action programmes being undertaken by the security forces. These include resettlement of the families and providing new avenues of economic engagement to the dependent family members, besides facilitating their education and healthcare. This is the core domain of the welfare function of the state. Healthy programmes of a permanent nature in this arena of public life help retain the confidence of the population that is still on the margin, particularly those who have not yet been weaned away by the adversaries. Such programmes should be configured to cater to the wider spectrum of rehabilitation situations, as part of damage control missions of the public authorities.

Efforts should also be made to bring back all those who have been won over by the adversary from the local grid and are working for them. The misguided people of the local habitat must be retrieved and put back into the main stream of society. Hence, congruent surrender-cum-rehabilitation schemes need to be designed in such a way that those who once surrender and join the scheme don't feel tempted to be recycled into the terror groups. The financial benefits and skill generation programmes for undertaking economic projects for sustenance need appropriate configuration, looking into the typicalities of the local environment. A selection of agencies for implementation is another crucial area to ensure the proper impact of the schemes. Involvement of NGOs could be fruitful from various angles, rather than keeping such projects totally in the official domains which nurture adverse rigidities. The rehabilitation programmes should be based on a cafetarian approach vis-a-vis the surendree, seeking his voluntary cooperation. The open ended collaborative approach may also prove to be effective. The combination of immediate and deferred benefits, along with periodic impact assessment and feedback linked up gradations could make such an initiative more value oriented. The idea is to sustain such programmes on the basis of core competencies and logistical support systems, which could be flexible and liberal, to evolve 'tailor made' packages in deserving cases. Experience shows that such schemes are often exploited by the politicking elements that are corrupt. Therefore, due caution has to be taken. From the operational angle, the motive and subsequent conduct of the surendree needs to be watched, lest it should amount to subversion through infiltration of recycled elements that are remotely controlled by the adversary. However, in this sabotage and counter sabotage game, various moves are to be scanned with caution and ways need to be found to filter those 'real' operatives who want to rejoin the main stream and are willing to cooperate in divulging relevant inputs.

The word of caution in such schemes remains the same. The zeal for one upmanship in multi-agency work environment or the statistical compulsions may generate reversals and hence be better, contained.

Media Management

Media management is based on trust, visibility and approachability. The various segments could be seen under the following task profile:

A: Media Relationship

- Have open-ended interface
- Promote Proactive interactions
- Establish constant mutual recognition
- Share information in media-friendly formats.

B: Media Propagation

- Issue timely press release in desired format
- Have focused interactions with print media
- Plan television and radio interviews
- Hold proper press conferences
- Write letters to editors on specific issues
- Develop television documentaries
- Release advertisements
- Monitor media propagation schedule, proper fillers and initiate rectifications, improvements

C: Visibility and Credibility Enhancement Exercises

- Regard public as the client with an open-collaborative approach and interactive-learning aptitude.
- Evolve as a service organization dedicated to ensure security and safety of the citizens.
- Ensure quick dissemination of information of incidents causing loss of life, property or generating a feeling of insecurity, educate public and seek their co-operation.
- Demonstrate value based positive behavior at the cutting-edge level to negate already branded police sub-culture as 'corrupt, high headed and repressive' in the eyes of the public.

D: Crystallize Delivery Mechanism

- Profiling higher management through "one-to-one media interaction", highlighting various issues.
- Organizing press visits to various places to highlight success stories.
- Issuing press releases whenever significant policy decisions are taken or a major event has taken place.
- Providing coverage of social responsibility activities.
- Highlighting individual achievements at the field level.
- Getting prepared short/longer duration documentaries and using them appropriately on television channels and also at various occasions.
- Providing creative inputs for preparation of brochures, pamphlets, diaries and calendars etc.

E: Managerial Profile of PR Team Head

- **Communication skill:** A trained person who understands the dynamics of modern media is essential for leading a PR effort of a large and complex organization. Since PR work involves 'selling' of ideas, a high level of communication skill is required by a PRO. One-to-one interactions and written outputs, both require an ability to express ones ideas clearly.
- **Inter-personal relations:** A 'public relations' job needs a person who can establish a good rapport with people – both journalists and officers of the organization. He must be able to generate trust in all.
- **Media rapport:** An honest and open relation with media is essential for a healthy PR operation. The level of trust and understanding between the PRO and 'beat' journalists should be of a high order. The access of the media to the PRO should be available on a 24x7 basis. All efforts should be made by the PRO to establish a long and meaningful relationship with journalists.
- **Vision and power of correlation:** A deep understanding of issues involved is necessary for PRO. Often the 'correct picture' is a matter of 'nuances'. Being aware of developments within the organization and society, and knowledge of 'trends' in the media thinking will enable the PRO to design his strategy in an effective manner. A nationalist, secular, modern and forward-looking attitude will get reflected in a healthy media image of the organization itself.

F: PR Team

PRO can best utilize his manpower by assigning specialized jobs like monitoring print media, visual media, coordinating inter-departmental stories etc., to individuals.

- A constant monitoring of newspapers and television channels is important. This work has to be assigned to a person who is trained and has an aptitude for this work.
- Administrative and housekeeping jobs are of a general nature and must be entrusted to persons who have the capability of handling file-work.
- Research & Development team to search for stories within the department and to portray the best available themes. This team needs to keep in touch with relevant individuals in the different branches for stories.
- Role of photographers is a very crucial aspect of print journalism. Normally newspapers have their photographers to cover events, but in-house photographers should also be used to supplement their efforts. High quality photographs from PR branch are sometimes used by magazines and newspapers. Similarly, video clippings can be shot by PR unit and provided to television channels.

G: Developing Work Culture with Inbuilt PR Skills

Each employee of the organization is the carrier of a positive image. Each person needs to be sensitized on this aspect during the course of training. This could be emphasized even during the senior officers' visit to field formations and also through periodical meetings. The work-culture needs to be built to identify the positive values of the organization and to suitably propagate them.

In the course of duty, troopers come in touch with the public at various points of time. At these moments of interaction, the image of an organization is built. Officers of various levels also have to interact with the media from time to time. Basic qualities of courtesy, good manners, honesty, and uprighteousness along with good communication skills will help to create a positive impression in the public.

Table - 9
Image Enhancement Activities : Check List
• Create and maintain media data bank.
• Work out content briefs/press release/exclusives.
• Extend media invitations and receive confirmations.
• Dissemination of information collaterals to media.
• Creation of story pegs.
• Facilitation of 'one to one' interactions between media and senior officials.
• Press visits.
• Media feedback.
• Outdoor propagation.
• Working out event-based PR coverage with media.
• Press conference.
• Preparation of documentary, video spots, photo gallery.
• Advertising and exhibitions.
• Publicity oriented 'Impact Features' through press & electronic media.
• Monthly magazines & special issues.
• Souvenirs, gifts on important occasions.
• Media training sessions for senior management.
• Creating cross-promotional opportunities.
• Maintaining press information link 'online'.
• Research & development on PR drives.

Psychological Operations

Psychological operations form a crucial part of perception management in high intensity conflict grids, as normal media may not be openly effective owing to the 'fear psychosis' generated by the terror groups. Open exposure by official circles may be constrained by many factors and suffer owing to a lack of outright approachability as well as credibility. Hence, resorting to 'psy ops' always pays.

The intrinsic features of 'psy ops' make it different from the branding exercises as seen above, though the extrinsic could be same or similar:

i) 'Psy ops' are based on covert modus operandi and there is no overt or direct visual depiction of the official agencies, the real think tank behind the campaign. The face boys are different. There could be different ways of such a masking, depending upon the typicalities of the conflict grid in terms of GTM, HTM and the cumulative responses.

ii) Third party interventions through Non Governmental Organizations (NGOs), are sought to undertake various direct as well as indirect projects to colour the perceptions and remove the pre-existing filters that distort reality.

iii) After due R&D the profile of such activities, as deemed relevant and appropriate for the local populace, is drawn and implemented in order to generate the desired cognitions. The co-relational and extrapolative exercises are crucial and could need the evaluation of purported psycho-behavioral strokes, through the visual formats so conceived for the area.

iv) Periodical reinforcers are needed to rebuild the perceptions, as indirect interventions through remotely controlled agencies as secret missions are likely to develop displacements and distortions. The initiative through local players could also be eclipsed by the fear of exposure of the 'masked agents'. There could also be a possibility of counter 'psy-ops' and hidden subversion.

v) Counter 'psy-ops' are very usual in such areas. The perception of fear is the leveraging factor for the terror groups. They have a local base which could be stronger than the base of security forces pumped in the area from remote places. The local language, customs, culture and day to day life style habits also matter a lot.

vi) Creation and sustenance of local support groups or leaders of such groups is also a much tried option. Use of official power to neutralize the opponent through ulterior strokes or circulation of money or other lucrative is rampant in sustaining such groups. The risk of double crossing definitely exists.

Respectable examples of 'psy ops' could be as under:

- Keeping scribes on payroll through hidden payments and seek favourable reports and articles.
- Asking third parties to organize TV and radio programmes, cultural shows, functions, etc., and convey indirect messages to mould the cognitions.
- Open blogs and sites on internet in a well masked manner for propagation.
- Involving third parties to use various media options to highlight atrocities and ill deeds of opponents. Publish and circulate books, pamphlets, posters against the opponent exposing them before the public.
- Open social service platforms, undertake such projects as drug de-addiction centres, through the NGOs and operate through them in order to generate positive sentiments and also to have reality feedbacks.

These operations have neither any limits nor any well defined permutations-combinations. The lesser evils are acceptable in these games in order to avoid the greater evils. One may also need to refrain from disclosing the ugly truths.

Chapter VI

Human Rights Windows

"The people who value privileges above principles soon lose both".

—Dwight Eisenhower

Human Rights (HR) assume critical significance in any civilized society. However, given the gradients of various vectors on a conflict grid at a given point of time, the operational response would be contingent upon various paradigms, which could be:

- operational rules of engagement imperative to neutralize a given violent situation.
- contextual legal empowerment to deal with such situations.
- possibility of resorting to non-kinetic means to handle the given situation.
- social tolerance level.

HR Concepts

Before locating such vectors on the operational matrix, it would be prudent to scan through the wide gamut of HR concepts. The domains of human rights have expanded from basic individual freedoms such as personal liberties, socio-cultural, political, religious and economic rights to progressive rights such as right to a safe environment, right to self development and self determination. The developed and under developed countries too present a vivid contrast in observing the minimum human rights, as they tend to differ in the level of social consciousness and other implicit values. Despite some variations, there is a general consciousness regarding human rights which revolves around human dignity and a healthy regard for humanity. It is a forward step to safeguard against any exploitation, humiliation, discrimination, deprivation or assault on personal liberties. However, there is also a growing debate on the issue of human rights of those who themselves perpetuate violence yet show a high disregard for the human rights of others. Under such situations, one can clearly perceive the claims for HR in any society depending upon the context of the struggle it is facing. Extended further, how can the HR concepts be formalised amidst an inequality of opportunity or choice. Although the advanced nations have been vociferous in propagating human rights, yet they are found to be no less active in violating the HR codes.

The UN codes on human rights, developed since 1948, pervade through all the aspects of a dignified and cultured human existence. Consequently, all the countries have legislated on the relevant HR issues and have created autonomous bodies to monitor such violations. The judicial agencies have also delivered landmark judgements on HR codes for various circumstances, particularly the HR issues during action taken by the police or security forces.

However, the HR concepts are not to be applied in a void. Hence, the socio-political sub optima gains relevance as they tend to shape the polity. The inequities tend to promote sharp divisive tendencies and various latent conflicts. When ideological legitimacies don't conform to social reality, distortions are bound to creep in, that give rise to undesirable demonstrative effects and system overloading. This further gives rise to a tendency of taking 'shortcuts' and 'window dressing', as people try to justify their actions which are otherwise marred by displaced perceptions and unreal consciousness. Hence, HR issues cannot be seen in isolation to the total environment, lest the causes be confused with the symptoms.

In operational situations, the approach must be people friendly, using minimum possible force and avoiding collateral damages. Restraint must be the key factor. Troopers need to be compassionate and nurture the people in their AOR to optimise the human resource. Observance of HR also means that a professionally planned offensive, based on specific operational inputs, should be launched so that no displacements should take place in the normal course. However, procedures of search, seizure and arrest need to be followed as per the laid down norms. Open, fair and transparent procedures should be followed with a high level of integrity. Proper audio-visual and documentary records should be maintained for any scrutiny. Any deviation from norms should be properly explained in the first information reports. Thus, the focus should be laid on a holistically synergised output.

HR SOPs

Certain standard operating procedures (SOPs) need to be evolved so as to avoid chances of any error. The relevant prohibitory orders, warning systems, power to use force, damage control drills, reporting systems are some of the important fields where it pays to have well defined SOPs which may assist in controlling the plausible deviations. The operational authorities must have cogent reasons to base their decision in invoking a given set of response or proaction. The Operational commander on the spot must also be 'satisfied' that it is necessary for the maintenance of the public order. Cooperation of various authorities should be sought as deemed necessary and as feasible. At the risk of being repetitive, it may be underlined that observance of legal mandates should be ensured. Specific reasons need to be noted down for any non observance, along with the required details.

Actions During Operations

- Ensure that use of force is essentially for maintenance of public order.
- Use minimum force required for effective action, under proper orders and under competent command levels.
- Use of force be initiated only after due warning in local language.
- Zero down on real trouble makers and incapacitate them by targeting on their lower limbs.
- Prevent harassment of any person or destruction of property to the extent possible.
- Proper records of all actions be maintained, in particular the inventories consumed in use of force and the circumstances necessitating the same.
- Injured persons should be properly attended to and necessary medical aid be ensured without any loss of time. Cogent response needs to be generated to take care of the dead bodies.
- Use various available technological options for

capturing any situation. Zero down on the problem areas. Generate real time digital records for self analysis as well as a judicial audit.

- Response in self defence has to be congruent and tenable.
- Search should be made to the extent possible in the presence of two respectable inhabitants of the locality.
- List of seizures be prepared and signed by the officer conducting the search and also the witnesses.
- Occupant of the premises or his nominee should be permitted to attend the search and also be given a copy of the seizure memo.
- Women be either separated, or if not so possible, be searched by another female with a strict regard to decency.
- Males under 15 yrs or females of any age be required to attend, to the extent possible, only at the place of residence of such a person.

After the operation, persons or property should be handed over to the local police station at the earliest, preferably within 24 hours. Reasons for delay beyond the permitted time need to be explained. Proper receipts of such handing over should be procured. Internal records should also be prepared well. Any incongruency should be duly explained. Medical relief needs to be provided to the injured and the ill. In case of the death of a person, the body needs to be handed over to the station officer incharge with details of the action taken along with a complete first information report. Circumstances leading to the death should be properly explained.

What should not be done?

1. Don't use excessive or indiscriminate force.
2. Don't keep a person in custody beyond bare minimum period, as permitted under the law, don't cause harassment otherwise.
3. Don't use third degree or torturous means.
4. Don't tamper with records.
5. Don't ill treat people, particularly women and children.
6. Don't inculcate or depict any communal bias.
7. Don't indulge in hand to hand struggle with civilians.
8. Don't accept rewards or gifts or donations.
9. Don't surrender or lose weapons to the enemy.
10. Don't ignore the importance of civil interface.

Zero Tolerance

In a nutshell, a deep respect for human rights along with a wide spread awareness amongst all ranks towards scrupulous upholding of the laws of the land has to appropriately evolve, in order to generate the right perceptions. It is an effective tool for healthy public relations in a civilian environment. Expeditious investigation of the HR allegations and congruent disposal enhances credibility. Responsible and effective forces have a 'Zero Tolerance' policy in human rights violations. However, an 'Iron fist in velvet gloves' is one of the doctrines that is more suitable in extreme conflict situations.

War of Perceptions

Since various power groups and stake holders operate in a conflict environment to promote their interests and cater to their hidden agenda, a bogey of HR issues may be raised as part of a 'war of perceptions'. It is then needless to say that in today's world of communications, a war of perceptions could be more fatal than a 'war of guns'. Varying responses are generated and manipulated through projections on the HR grid, highlighting the deeds of the troopers, thereby inflicting aspersion on those in power. At times, the allegations are true, at times they are manipulated. At times, it may be difficult to draw a line of difference between the due and the sundue, as violence may necessitate counter violence to neutrilize a situation. The right of self defence may also be subjected to a detailed scrutiny through varied lenses. There may also be situations where the lesser evils have to be accepted to avoid the greater evils. Hence, the HR norms, which are followed in the normal course of events, may not hold good in extreme situations of conflict. Here, surgical interventions appear to be the only course of action.

The onus, therefore, falls on those at the helm of affairs to ensure that legal powers are not put to any misuse and the larger public interest remains the deciding factor. Bonafide acts could be viewed under the protection clause. However, no mercy needs be shown to those operating with malifed intentions and knowingly violating the given norms. Public onus and troopers' morale could be the two extreme yardsticks between which the HR issues may oscillate. At times, it may be politically incorrect to admit the truth. At times, bureaucratic tangles may dominate. The truth on the ground and truth on paper may present glaring contrasts. Political and public lobbying, media management and psychological operations may play a crucial role in keeping any happenings under wraps.

On the spot questioning during an ongoing operation and a post operation detailed interrogation may differ in their intrinsic, entailing different approaches. With scientific aids and more behavioral techniques, there is an increasing realization to abstain from using physical torture. It is preferable to prompt a person to voluntarily divulge all the details he has in his mind, rather than augmenting an escape – avoidance response, which could be quite distorted.

Thus bonafide and judicious use of force in the larger public interest holds the key. Notwithstanding the judicial pronouncements and NHRC guidelines, the operational facts need to be properly documented at each stage to withstand any legal scrutiny.

CHAPTER VII

LEADERSHIP AND MANAGEMENT OF CHANGE

"Great deeds are usually wrought at great risks".

—Herodotus

Leadership Vision

'Tread carefully and lead cheerfully' is the age old advice of successful operational commanders. To lead efficiently as well as to wield the rod effectively is a monumental task. To successfully direct and monitor both, the professional and to some extent the personal, facets of one's subordinate's life is a dream secretly nurtured by the commanders. However, it is a dream not so easily realized as it requires sustained effort in order to develop a healthy, mutually trusting environment with a meaningful relationship that augments achievement orientation towards the aforesaid goals.

Those in command need to predetermine the objective with a visionary approach. They need to enforce a code of conduct and a direction to be adopted, simultaneously setting a precedent for their subordinates through exemplary, modular and supportive behaviour. The culture of the organization is, thus, considerably dependent on the projected role models which necessitates the natural activation of the intervention procedure to be successfully conducted by those in authority.

Management and Leadership

Management and leadership, though having distinctive characteristics, are still the flip sides of the same coin. Despite having clear cut distinctions, they are functionally integrative in nature in an optimally moulded organization. They have certain common reference points which cannot and should not be ignored before we venture into their complex concepts, such as the gravity of 'common functional goals'. The organizational goals should carry with them a common converting factor between the individual requirements and the individual's aspirations. However, generally, the former manages to take precedence over the latter.

In the public service organizations, especially the 'security forces', values are distinctly different. Here the organizational objectives along with the personal needs, desires and aspirations hold little relevance vis-à-vis the national and social cause. Leadership influences monitoring the nobler values may, thus, successfully generate a demonstration effect inducing in the subordinate the right momentum and inspiration to perform for a greater and a wider cause. Leadership, therefore, eulogises self sacrifice, self denial and abstinence inspiring a similar trend in those that look upto the hierarchy for guidance and ideal manifestation. This is what we call the internalized approach. In contrast is the externalist approach where the higher command sets non-flexible goals, seeks absolute compliance and ruthlessly hauls up the juniors for a substandard performance. An over ambitious manager who directs all his actions and energies towards career upliftment alone will sooner or later be identified and find himself at the receiving end of hostility.

Ability and professional efficiency minus integrity has become unacceptable today. The days of colonial legacy are now history. On the other hand, in today's world a healthy mix of appropriate values may well see successful implementation of organizational objectives and leave the individual in a more blissful, satisfied and peaceful state. Public service officers are, in fact, blessed with an enviable state of pursuing a meaningfully enriched life style, along with ensuring the upliftment of those working under them. Despite the unfair comparisons often made between the private and public services, the public servant wins hands down, having the noble opportunity to serve selflessly, to become an ideal role model and to bear the satisfaction that they have made the right difference to those under them and to society at large. It is here that they can proudly claim to perceive themselves as true and befitting leaders.

To deserve, rather than to forcefully extract respect and obedience from one's subordinates is the true hallmark of an ideal commander. This is what forms the crux of a true and able leadership. Leadership based on total acceptance knows no subordinates, no power and no arm-twisting techniques. Authority alone cannot compare with the humane and behavioral excellence of a leadership based on the dogmas of professional and personal uniqueness. In today's complex scenario, the 'know-how' and 'do-how' paradigms must include a keenly developed 'think-how' as well, in order to ideally meet the surrounding human sensitivities. Taking a wider and a long term perspective, with the subsequent rise in the hierarchy, technical abilities are to a great extent replaced by managerial acumen and these gradually give way to behavioral expertise.

Client Relationship

It is actually the art of 'client-relationship' which helps realize the degree of acceptance rather than a 'master-servant' relationship. It is the 'pursued process' rather than the sole concentration on the task at hand that eventually enables rich dividends. As a responsible public servant we owe it i.e., we are under a moral obligation to provide due satisfaction to our 'client' which is the society at large. That for the deserving is the eventual litmus test as all our actions should be geared towards ensuring the well being of the society that we have taken up cudgels to serve.

Command Tools

However, the most efficient and dynamic commander cannot give befitting results unless supported by the appropriate tools that are in congruence with the mission at hand. Let us delve into features of the desired tools a commander must use for success. The ability to define and predict the course of growth and development is one of the true characteristics of strategic management. This accompanied with a professional focus further strengthens the cause of interpretation i.e., maintaining professional ethics, genuine care and concern for the public welfare, ensuring the upliftment and the required development of the masses, professional ability and integrity, technological adaptability that keeps pace with the advancement in the system and, of course, making the desired valuable contributions to the given cause.

The ability to maintain ruthless objectivity i.e., to rise above ones subjective attitudes, likes and dislikes regarding caste, creed and religion, with no communal bias is another basic characteristic of true leadership. To rise above the 'self' is highly desirable, but then it is equally difficult to do so, as somewhere along the way one may either come under the influence of the opportunists or may surrender to one's personal jealousies, hatred, anger, fury and prejudices, thereby compromising on the very intrinsics on which effective leadership is dependent and balanced.

The ability to decipher, perceive and innovate in real time is another key tool to success. Going by tactical intuitions, monitoring an action without putting it through the mundane reasoning and analysis is the key 'Success Mantra'. It is the ability to accurately perceive the battle times either through the experience gained during insurgency, realistic war games or even through case studies, simulated exercises, reading material, etc., that ensures success.

The moral ability to defer and the moral courage to decline in case of a trade-off or deviance gives equal impetus to one's commander status. The non-feasible and the non-ethical should not be succumbed to. We may develop the ability to counsel in a balanced yet a motivating manner with an enlightened and proper understanding of the human mind and psyche, seriously imbibed through detailed inroads into the issues at hand, this is possible through experience, along with an active participation on the job at hand. This may lead to a high level of orientation and would properly enable us to guide, share, ensure healthy habits and induce professional power amongst our subordinates.

Simple Living

The most vital, yet unfortunately the most neglected, aspect is the concept of 'simple living'. The critical importance of this leadership tool can be evidently eulogized via the realm of history. 'Spartans' at the height of their military success sent a deputation to the Oracle at Dolphin and demanded arrogantly, "Can anything threaten Sparta?" 'Yes, luxury', came the humble reply. There lies the major secret of a public servant's success. To follow a frugal and austere lifestyle sets an ideal for the force to ape and follow, thereby helping to mitigate so many related vices namely - greed, corruption, disharmony, dissatisfaction, disorderliness, indiscipline and the like. An ostentatious lifestyle, thus, can be declared as not being an option for the public servant. However, this need not be confused with shabbiness and a drab and unkept appearance along with maintaining a sub-standard life style. Dignity of appearance is an essentiality and must under no given circumstances be ignored. Similarly, over-familiarity with one's subordinates may actually result in insubordination and indiscipline. A correct balance is imperative and has to be maintained to ensure a wholesome personality.

Leadership Continuum

Before switching over to the specifics of operational leadership, the various generalities of leadership continuum may be summarized as below.

A leader is one who, gradually fades away into the background himself. But, he raises the efficiency level of his juniors to take on complex tasks and responsibilities, develop clarity of thought and objective, a clear focus on the path to traverse and become spiritually elevated to the extent that work itself becomes worship and their ultimate goal. Command management calls for ability of foresight, vision, pro-action, analysis to manage change and optimization of capability. An intense belief in humanity results in providing the positive, encouraging strokes to achieve and progress rather than create negative vibes through persistent acrimonious behaviour. The idea is to 'win hearts' and not immobilize them with raw terror. He moulds their fate, leads them, yet he is one of them. He needs to rise above the status of a 'paper tiger' and achieve as well as motivate through 'smart efforts', not just sweat and onerous toil. If the juniors repose their blind trust in him, his work is already more than half done, as compliance of his directions and acceptance of his ability to direct and guide is never challenged, but enthusiastically aped and complied with. It is the aura of his personality that ensures and determines the compliance of his decision and viewpoint, rather than the orders issued on paper. To ensure all round positive results, the focus needs to be on prompting them to do right in a win-win situation rather than attempting to catch them doing wrong in a no-win situation.

The leadership continuum may appear something like this:

Chart - 5

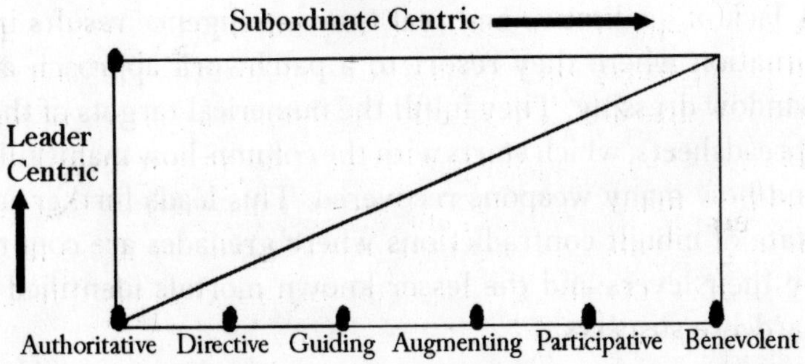

The above spectrum is suggestive of the various leadership styles which may be adopted, depending upon the following factors –

- Personal traits of the team commander.
- Intrinsic categorization of team members.
- Nature of the situation.

Whereas authoritative leadership provides no discretion to those being led, benevolent leadership focuses on the self actualized involvement and autonomy on the part of the subordinates. In between these two extremes, there may be several variations.

Police operations may, however, present a different picture. Hence, it is often reiterated that one should proceed from practice to theory and not vice-versa.

Leadership and Police Sub-Culture

There is a famous quotation – "If you don't know which road to take, then any road will take you there". Sooner or later one has to confront this fact rather than escape it forever. The scenario would be more appropriately assimilated when we take a kaleidoscopic view of the security operations and the intrinsic base for such ops. It is presumed that security agencies would launch their operations based on hard actionable intelligence and meticulously perform pin pointed surgery to the extent required. But reality eludes such expectations. The sub-culture in which the security agencies keep rolling suffers from certain displacements. A lack of qualitative and real time intelligence results in a situation where they resort to a patchwork approach and window dressing. They fulfill the numerical targets of their spreadsheets, which starts with the column-how many killed and how many weapons recovered. This leads further to a state of inbuilt contradictions where grenades are counted by their levers and the lesser known mortals identified as hardcore suspects.

The question of human rights then gains sanctity and the presence of the security force becomes more of a necessary evil, as perceived by an independent viewer. Secondly, the chemistry of security forces undergoes drastic changes, so often in so many ways, that its 'course of journey' always remains subject to trial and error. The policing sub-culture is never able to draw a synthesis with the diplomatic sub-culture and vice-versa. One would agree that any social conflict, however acute, would always need a diplomatic peace approach. The hard line approach through security agencies can only contain it for a while. How much and how long would be the duration of the bitter pill often remains subject to prolonged audit and criticism unless history becomes too remote to be retrieved and recollected. The mathematics of such an approach where the differentials do not support integration, or vice-versa, makes the human calculus indeterminate. Answers are then found in matching the deficiency with increasing the numbers or demands for technological upgradation without remembering the fact that both the courses affect the work output in more ways than one. Whatever we may do, but without a clear road map, even a high-tech vehicle with more soldiers to ride on it could take us anywhere, but not necessarily where we need to go. It, therefore, goes without saying that optimum congruency at the organizational level amidst its cognitions, visions and operations has to be attained to draw maximum synergetic advantage. This aspect is important also from the viewpoint that the police organizations are often affected by the external environment created by fluid diplomacy. Internally, the congruency level is low owing to the inherent conflicting subculture in police functioning that gives rise to a series of paradoxes.

Amidst Intangibles

During crisis situations the models which have succeeded are not the ones which can be compared with peacetime standards that have the zeal to have a 'Zero level' of defiance from the regular norms. The irony of such role and goal conflicts often lingers on, as the law enforcing agencies are required to explain every tangible occurrence while they are not allowed to take any credit for the intangibles. Often we don't preach what we practice, nor do we openly admit or propagate what really works in counter insurgency. It is the non-visual policing in the secret mode through STF or SOG or CATS which has often worked following the age old policies of Saam (trust & faith), Daam (monetary temptations), Dand (coercion or fear of corporal punishment), Bhed (divide and rule by taking advantage of differences and frictions). We teach the theory to evolve the practice, whereas workable practices should evolve the theoretical principles of work.

In an outstretched socio-political set up where the list of frictions and divisions have a tendency to multiply multifold, day after day, peace can become a rare commodity. Peace is generally restored in installments at a huge price. The job of peace keepers in such situations may swerve from the sub-normal to the abnormal, calling for surgical interventions as a part of contingency management. The superficially perceived reality of society also induces certain contradictions compelling the security agencies to evolve a work culture which is congruent with their need to manage various 'urgencies', amidst the existing time and resource constraints. Community could prove to be a major support in such a situation. Therefore, the relevance of the catalytic role of the police in providing material services to the society, in order to win over their hearts and minds, has found its way as against the singular role of checking the people for their deviant behavior. This has also brought forward the humane face of the security forces and provided an opportunity to showcase their behavioral sensitivities along with the communal acceptance. Hence, the inbuilt social mechanism comes into play as a force multiplier. We must not overlook the fact that the grotesquely apathetic behavior of people sends forth a wave of repugnance that in turn breeds extreme criminal responses.

Commandments for OPS Leadership

The lessons from operational experience can now be theorized to generate certain postulates which can be called the commandments for operational leadership:

- Commander should be capable of scanning the environment, given its volatility, ambiguity, uncertainty and complexities.

- He should make a correct operational assessment in a due consultative manner.
- He should be having organizational capabilities to integrate heterogeneous components of combat resources.
- He should be a master in augmenting the synergetic response of his team members as well as other agencies working in the area through the right strokes.
- He should evolve and operationalise good intelligence network.
- He should be capable of mitigating the attritions in his force and evolve the capacity to cope with the subversions and sabotage.
- He should be competent enough to manage the time differential in generating counter capabilities with renewed learning and technological support.
- He must not overlook the rules of operational engagement for various situations, at any point of time.
- He must also know the art of perception management and devise his strategies to handle the media.
- He must focus upon winning the heart and mind of the people, clearly demarcating 'who is not the enemy'.
- He must draw a clear flow of accountability for various tasks.
- Stress management and morale keeping should be his top priority i.e.:
  - He must keep cool.
  - He must motivate his team to deliver with precision.

- He must lead by example and be a role model.
- He must maintain combat worthiness of his troops.
- He must gain an advantage over adversaries through an expression of gut, guile and professional response.
- He must teach his troopers how to win silently and face set backs stoically and with bravery.

- He must be sensitive, responsive, decisive, progressive and possess a high level of integrity as well as loyalty.

Process of Change

The most important management trait of a successful leader is to develop a realistic vision and focus upon an inherent process of change to evolve congruent organizational response capabilities as well as augment the human resource development.

The process of change involves the following steps:

- Carrying a SWOT analysis i.e., determining strengths, weaknesses, opportunities and threats under the dynamic environment and drawing a comparative profile.
- Determine likely response capacity deficits and the areas needing change.
- Ascertain the nature and quantum of change required in organizational structure, human resource arenas, infrastructural and logistical supports, technological upgradations and domains necessary to generate the required synergy.
- Unfreeze the older patterns and responses.
- Initiate the new change as per the congruent modules.

- Refreeze the new patterns and learnings.
- Provide periodic reinforcements.

The generalities of management of change, when translated in operational terms, would definitely entail us to evolve comparative grading for hardware, software and 'thoughtware'. Whereas hardware and software options can be congruently evaluated by a team of experts arriving at the appropriate configurations and the cost benefit implications on a given time scale, the management of 'thought ware' is not only crucial but also critical. Ushering in the desired change in the 'organic' component of any organization is really a great leadership challenge. How to convince people to feel the need for a change, how to neutralize their old habits, how to generate new learning, how to mould the neo-behavioral response and how to deal with the emerging conflicts owing to a lack of capability are some of the relevant issues which ought to be addressed by those at the helm of affairs.

Learning Environment

Now the question still remains how to go about it in the 'arid zone' of performance that, more often than not, oscillates at low equilibrium levels. To determine the job performance what we need is not just an isolated factor of skills but also the factor of commitment which happens to be of equal importance It has been found that commitment is a more crucial vector on the performance scale. A committed soldier would develop his indigenous software by a simple trial and error method. A non-committed worker even though having high skills, may jump the 'bail' and even escape getting caught. The whole discussion leads us to appreciate two formats of learning-the 'commitment-arousal learning' and the 'skill formation learning'. It has been observed through a study of successful organizations that:

- The best learning environment is provided on the job where the role of a "key post holder" and the "peer group" is important.
- 'Autonomy' to work along with a 'value' of the decisions taken at a rank keeps the spark alive for better commitment.
- Informal and direct interactions are more effective than communication through 'paper shots'.
- Catch them doing right is a better approach than catch them doing wrong.
- A sense of inequity often leads to conflicts.
- There ought to be enough space for creativity (via decentralization) and error tolerance. Let people be prompted to commit errors, as much and as early as possible, to know their real worth and their scope for improvement.

Human Relationship Management

The critical observations, as made above, highlight the need to focus on "leadership evolution" at the top and middle levels. It is more so required in view of the focus gradually shifting from Human Resource Development (HRD) to Human Relationship Management (HRM). It is proved by empirical facts that silent communications control 80% of our behavioral responses owing to the strong demonstration effects. Working under creative and conducive conditions in itself is a motivator and an intrinsic mobilizer. The exclusive dependence on extrinsic factors in terms of extra pay or diet, beyond a point, ushers in distorted learning. The intrinsic quality of human resource does matter. The policing jobs, otherwise too, require a high level of response-sensitivity in the individual.

Synergetic Work Culture

The exclusive specializations often pose a problem of co-ordination and collective performance. One agency tends to find fault in the other in order to account for their failures. Hence the 'compact' character of the teams should not be overlooked. Secondly, the essential skills for work performance have to be endowed on each and every member of the group. It is prudent not to overlook the skill categorizations in the form of technical, managerial and behavioral skills so as to understand their workable combinations, which are congruent with empirical utility rather than theoretical perceptions.

Eventually, it is necessary not only to demarcate the area for learning but also the areas of viable work culture. To cite relevant examples, let us consider "area dominance" drills. Some of us delve seriously upon the actions to be taken only after we have left the camp on a mission. Whereas one would agree that 80% of the task needs to be completed before we leave the camp i.e., analysis of past inputs, selection of sites or targeted areas, activity analysis for the operation, etc. In that case, only 20% remains to be done in the field. Good wars are first won across the table. Strategic planning is, therefore, important. We can consider more situations where cognitive clarity becomes a casualty. The troops generally move out in uniform so their position is easily visible. In case it is a trip without actionable intelligence, the risk becomes more than the likely gains. We do not even make use of such exercises to build up an initial proper database. Walking on foot and inviting a chance encounter is taken to be synonymous to 'Gasht'. Intelligence generation, as part of a well planned 'Gasht', covert or overt, is altogether a different ball game. One has to work genuinely to earn community trust. We may choose the necessary targets who can be motivated by money to fetch actionable intelligence.

One may have to become a strategist to derive advantage from the frictional groups and aggrieved elements or follow the manipulative policies of divide and rule. This calls for patience, behavioral skills and dexterity. At the risk of being repetitive, it is reiterated that covert policing is more important than overt or visual policing. Similarly, law and order policing may require a larger strength of the troops but counter-insurgency operations may face difficulties with a larger group strength, so much so that there may arise problems of cohesiveness, fire control coordination and controlled movement. Work parameters are often different. To cite another example, civic action programmes are generally oriented towards putting up a onetime grand show and a publicity hype rather than ensuring a gradual, meaningful and tangible assistance to the community with a view to win the trust of the "soldiers without uniform" who would then willingly assist the "social watch dogs" in uniform. One knows the ways but ideal implementation is hampered by bureaucratic audit trails calling for a dot-to-dot compliance.

The silent communications of the 'defacto' work culture overpowers the 'dejure'. Hence, there ought to be some congruency between the two. Accordingly, the training programmes could be suitably configured. What calls the shots? Isn't the learning on the job moulding our response patterns? Have we evolved the desired road map? Do we know the path we need to tread? This is not a one time or a one day process. It is a constant and a dynamic exercise.

Each time a new optima shall evolve, as the technologies advance and the situations change. But we cannot overlook the human factor where the actual "copability" lies. The holistic 'defacto' work culture largely influences the intrinsic character of the coveted copability through silent communication, which is far more potent. Without "copability" we may be dressed 'hi-tech' but may miss out on our mission as we may not know where we should be heading. If we can achieve this, NOWHERE will then transform into NOW HERE!

CHAPTER VIII

STRATEGIC VISION (TACTICAL LEADERSHIP)

"Study the past if you would define the future".

—Confucius

This facet of the asymmetric warfare thrives on such codes that are unwritten yet often swing the balance between success and failure. These are the codes which go much beyond the conscientious leadership influences which we have seen in the preceding chapter. These are the codes which open new vistas of tactical leadership, as the tactical moves are decided on the basis of the SWOT analysis of the adversary. This is a strategic shift from the blind self to the open self. For the sake of clarity, we may call it a shift from managerial leadership to tactical leadership. It marks the difference between efficiency and effectiveness. It underlines the shift of focus from first person to the third person and the corresponding change in tactical norms, congruent with the cunningness of the opponent. It is sustained on the age old dictum that 'everything is fair in love and war'. What is tangible in such a game could be far from the truth. It is a game of the intangibles and the invisibles.

Systems Approach

In general parlance, strategy could mean dealing with the systemic sustenance amidst the turbulences of the external environment with a proactive vision. The futuristic road map is so well conceived that nothing is left to a chance which can elude reality. The systems approach, as understood in management terminology, has various processes and flows which are integrally channelized to optimize the synergetic output:

- That any system is a part of a larger system which determines its external environment and the degree of external linkages with other co-systems.
- The external environment is multifaceted and highly turbulent.
- The given system is itself constituted of various sub systems which act and react on each other, thus determining the holistic characteristics of the system in aggregate.
- The inputs of a system are always greater than the output. This negative entropy depicts the condition of sustenance.
- The system has an inbuilt capacity to find a minimum sustenance level in any turbulent condition and to recover to an extent. This homeostatic property constitutes the intrinsic strength.

The understanding of a system in terms of the above properties lends us new filters to focus upon the constituent subsystems and derive various 'permutation-combinations' to enhance the level of synergy. This strategic vision, when applied to the security set up, would help the commander to develop new external as well as internal perspectives. The inter dependence of various sub systems, when viewed from the micro and semi macro domains, would help develop better insight. The responses of various stakeholders at the grass root level then can be appreciated, and more appropriate reinforcers can be planned to bring in the desired changes. Then the 'ownership' realization can also set in.

The external environment is highly competitive. The conflicts and frictions emanating from such an environment entails a study of the network on which rivalries thrive. The principles of system analysis can also be applied to realize the exact positives and negatives of the opponent. A proper analysis of various ingredients also helps to predict the strategic moves of the opponent. The world has witnessed various wars and sub-wars. Great generals have evolved various ground rules and covert tactics. We can also arrive at the same junctures and locate the roads leading to the targeted destinations. The system analysis helps us to widen our vision and see the integrated whole as a system in aggregate as well as a sub system of a larger whole. Having done that, various flows can be well synthesized to draw out an effective combat matrix. The cognitive model needs no further elaboration for those who are already in the business of commanding successful operations. We can now talk of the operational specifics as part of strategic vision for those who need a checklist to appreciate the underlying wisdom.

Operational Insights

The art of 'Geographical terrain' as well as 'Human terrain' mapping is the basic prerequisite. These concepts have already been discussed in the preceding chapters. It will suffice here to reiterate the following golden rules -

- Know the place better than the local residents.

- Know the people better than own mother.

As in a game of chess, one has to be on a constant vigil and move, beating the enemy at his own game. One has to keep a little ahead of the enemy in tactical planning and keep discovering 'profitable ways' of engaging the opponent in asymmetric war.

The writings of shrewd generals often indicate such tactics. One such smart move is, 'load only war material on the shoulders of the troopers and make sure you don't burden them with any administrative stock; instead snatch the administrative requirements from the opponent'. Resource planning and ease of movement are the strategic decision points here. Similarly, there are psycho-behavioral tips, 'raise anger in the soldiers to consolidate offensives on the opponent' and 'balance the performance with positive strokes and rewards'. The morale and motivational factors are the relevant parameters here as part of the core strategy. Not merely this, but rules also point out that those captured from amongst the opponent group should be treated kindly as they could become a source of useful information and operational inputs. Thus, one can enhance one's strength vis-a-vis the enemy.

An excellent combat matrix is one which can facilitate the breaking of the resistance of the opponent without a fight. There could be different strategic moves in such a game. One should clearly know where the big teams would be needed for success and where the small teams would work better. Most of the asymmetric war situations favor small team operations. Such teams should be compact, well equipped and well linked. The Commander should also consider the combat variants while taking decision on the constitution and configuration of the teams:

- Do we need the teams for creating deception?

- Should there be an attack by the opponent, what shall be the autonomous counter response?
- Should the first attack be made by us, what shall be the well networked configurations keeping in mind the killing zone, escape routes and counter deception, etc.?
- What shall be the configuration of troops sent for supplementing the main combat force?

Strategic OPS Grid

One of the crucial misunderstandings at the level of the commanding officers is not being able to differentiate between the operational tasks and the administrative flows. Operations on administrative principles will result in arousing a feeling of restlessness in the troops and dampen their morale. Operations are based on optimizing the opportunities as and when they come, without getting entangled in the administrative cobwebs. Operations are based on the principle of flexibility whereas administrative norms promote rigidities. Hence, one has to have a clear strategic operational vision. Operations need not be constrained by administrative tangles. Even the choice of a right person at the right place may be based on operational evaluation and not on the administrative norms of service tenure, administrative performance reports, etc. The Principle of adaptability is relevant for operations. It is interesting to know the categorization of people and how they make operational decisions. A wise person, a true intellectual, focuses on establishing his merit. A brave person harps on his courage. A covetous commander seizes upon an advantage. A stupid leader who has no fear of death prompts his troopers to rush in without any proper assessment. In essence, one must know when to fight and when not to fight. Observe a cat's adept moves in cornering a rat. Despite being big and strong, she does not make her move; instead, she awaits the opportunity that comes along with zero failure. One must know how to handle various types of opponents, superior as well as the inferior. Even an inconsequential opponent may taste success if he is well prepared, spirited as well as tactful. It all depends on how focused one is and how timely are one's plans to attack the opponent just when the latter is least prepared to repel.

Strategic Operational Grid: Impact analysis

	⟶	A	B
↓	**Options**	**Know the opponent**	**Dont know the opponent**
1.	Know your own Combat potentials	Confidence	Suspicion
2.	Do not know your own combat potentials	Apprehension	Hopelessness

Table - 10

The above grid shows four situations emerging out of the two options each on either side marked as 1, 2 and A, B. The likely combat situations are depicted in the corresponding grid. This is only a thought provoking exercise. There may be innumerable impact-analysis variants amidst these broad categorizations.

Given the above grid formulations and the corresponding situations, various tactical inferences flow out. Detailed enumerations on the related issues could be avoided for the sake of brevity and one can straight away zero down upon the tactical dispositions.

Tactical Dispositions

It is wise to win through operational skills rather than relying on sheer strength. There should be no aimless movement or purposeless attacks. It not only tires the troops but also exposes them to avoidable risks. In fact, any combat planning should be done across the 'table' before leaving the camp. It should be based on all the relevant data and plausible parameters. One must assess the opponent's intentions, plan the strategies with complete secrecy and then counter his moves. Operational movements should be quite surreptitious. In fact, tactical movements and dispositions need to be duly concealed to generate an element of surprise and deception. Securing oneself is in ones own hands, whereas an opportunity to defeat is provided by the opponent.

The next important aspect is to optimize the use of the available response capacity. Strategic rationality would suggest such options which would give a greater result for a lesser effort. Lay traps and 'lure' your enemy into it. Follow the combat tactics of the 'weak and the strong' points of manipulation. One can indulge in indirect offensives, rather than direct attacks. One need not rush in all the time, but choose to rapidly evolve. Merit rating and team building concepts could be adopted to configure such synergetic contingents which could successfully confuse the opponent and keep him on the move. Certain age old combat tactics for guerilla warfare could be relevant in this context:

- Map the likely critical situations.
- Conduct 'SWOT' analysis of the opponent, besides that of self.
- Follow the line of least resistance in moving.
- Foresee opponent's attack points, like in a game of chess.

- Expose opponents' dispositions.
- Emerge from void, strike at vulnerable points, attack at unexpected hours and avoid well defended places of the opponent for such offensives.
- Make timely use of 'bluffs' and 'deceptions'.
- Cut off lines of communication and supply.
- Ambush like a cat.
- Master the art of lying low or reversing for a better opportunity.

Art of Planned Deviations

Experience shows that deviations and manipulations are at the base of converting an opportunity into a tactical advantage. It will not be out of place if one were to term it as the 'art of planned deviations'. This is essential to avoid the traps being laid by the opponent and skip his counter offensives. Hence, one must master the art of studying the circumstances minutely and scanning through the relevant operational inputs. This can help in rebuilding one's combat strength and streamlining the available resources. This would also prevent a situation where one unknowingly swallows the 'bait' offered by the opponent. Before each operational move, it would be desirable to undergo 'one minute mental rehearsal' and assess the likely risks. One can accordingly manipulate the geographical and human terrain inputs to draw upon an advantage. The timings of counter-moves could also be factored in. In fact, the study of the moods and modus-operandi of the adversary is the crux here. One can assail the opponent's mental equilibrium, create a 'hub' in the enemy domain and retain self possession. Futile exercises or forced movements should be avoided to conserve energy as well as retain the morale, besides avoiding undue exposure. The whole success depends upon 'moving ahead of the opponent' in all these tactics and enticing him wherever possible. Whenever well geared to attack, then attack at the speed of 'lightning'. Create a 'thunder' at the opportune moment, if so deemed necessary. The best course would be to lead the opponent on to a given escape route where he can be easily neutralized.

The analysis of the circumstances, as indicated above, could be done on the basis of a grid analysis –

- How well one knows his opponent?
- How much one understands the combat circumstances?
- How much one has developed deep insights into geographical and human terrain?
- How much one really knows about his own configurations, including the human resources?
- Are we proactive or reacting in desperation?

It is a war of variance which makes the difference. Fighting for small gains could be foolish as one faces the risk of undue exposure. Thus, the cost-benefit of operational variances have their own rationale and are beyond any administrative realm. The risk analysis would hover around an opportunity gain to self and an opportunity loss to the opponent. In fact, much would depend on the following conditions:

- What are the limiting factors to our response capacity?
- What are the time constraints?
- What is the opportunity cost of letting the opponent escape or survive?
- What is the operational advantage of any offensive planned against the opponent?

One of the substitutive strategies, in place of direct confrontation, could be to weaken and sublimate the opponent. Psychological operations provide such windows of intervention. A war of perception and disgruntlement within could do much more than expected, if one can really play one's cards well. The efficacy of these tactics is not directly controllable, as such moves can be effectively thwarted by the opponent through his hold on the human terrain of the conflict grid.

Operationally, one has to constantly look for the footprints of the opponent and keep scanning the surroundings for the same. Such footprints could be both visible as well as invisible. Virtually, the good commanders have to place themselves on a higher echelon to build a capacity of constant effective scanning. Enemy's operational terrain could be narrow, inaccessible, complicated, elusive and snarled up in varying degrees. In order to succeed in a crisis, it is essential to keep oneself updated during peace time.

Command Capabilities

The choice of a right commander is a must. He has to be over and above any of the following command deficits-

- Carelessness
- Rashness
- Cowardice
- Partiality and discrimination
- Over protection
- Fear of criticism

The commander with the above disqualifications is likely to lead his team to a definite failure. Operational experience shows certain surest ways to fail. What are they?

- Neglecting SWOT analysis of the opponent.
- Lack of peace time capacity building.
- Lack of delegation of authority at the cutting edge level.
- Blind eye to indiscipline.
- Lack of merit rating and congruent task assignment.
- Unjustifiable anger.

We can, for the sake of cognitive clarity and extrapolation, think of a 'Susceptibility Grid' as follows:

		Opponent	
		Not open to attack	**Open to attack**
Self	Not ready to attack	Lack of combat capability	Loss of combat opportunity
	Ready to attack	Difficult combat situation	Ideal combat situation

Susceptibility Grid

Table –11

In fact strategic leadership and the art of combat should be viewed as the core business of the commanders. Constant shift of plans and places, as per the dynamic character of the conflict grid, could be the desired option in extreme situations. Standard operating procedures should be followed for various operational moves. However, an opponent should be sensibly accommodated till you reach a position to effectively crush him. Owing to statistical pressure and a lack of operational vision, the security forces often defy these principles and tend to provide a tactical advantage to the adversary through their premature dispositions. Whereas, one needs to be alert to the traps being laid by the opponent, including the allurements offered by him, efforts should be continuously made to locate a strategic entry into his domain, in order to neutralize him.

The Commanders ought to win over their subordinates through their authority, good faith and a rewarding attitude. Thus, they can maintain their control, cohesiveness and a high quality of delivery of their services. Good commanders don't wear out their troops unnecessarily. They don't send their troops on operations unless they can forsee an advantage. They don't use the troops mechanically, nor do they leave the responsibility of deployment on unconcerned subordinates. 'Use not the troops unless you see a gain' and 'fight not unless you occupy a critical position'; such are the strategic dispositions good commanders follow. They know the job, they know their people, they know the circumstances, they know the moves of the opponent, they can predict contingencies and, thus, give an effective combat plan at the appropriate time to their subordinates, who will then be highly motivated to perform in a compact, cohesive manner. Strategic operational vision hovers around all these crucial dimensions. However, it is a game of wit where baits, bluffs and manipulations are used to find ways to success. It is a game where the lesser evils are adopted to avoid the greater evils, but only when it is unavoidable and only to the extent that it is indispensable. Strategically, one need not rejoice in a victory, nor grant any explanation for a defeat. Asymmetric warfare hinges between the tangibles and intangibles. Tangibly, the counter terrorism responses have to be humane and within the legal norms, taking care of the local sentiments. Intangibly, such responses cannot afford to neglect the undercurrents and, therefore, devise covert counter moves to regulate the flow of such undercurrents, in terms of direction as well as magnitude.

Synthesis

All said and done, various stake holders in a conflict situation have multifaceted interests, some are seemingly genuine, some ulterior. There could be many permutations and combinations in an unbounded situation where no linear solutions are available. The intricacies of conflict matrix may delay all the known rules of synthesis or integration. Hence, security considerations call for the initiation of such measures which fall in the 'domain of secrecy', legitimatized by the sovereign supremacy within the well defined specific-norms. Use of sources, agents and spies, as eyes and ears, are a much coveted option for attaining the desired quality output. However, such options are fraught with dangers. One should not dare to play this game unless one has mastered the art of tackling this game. It is like moving on a tight rope maintaining 'a knife edged balance'.

CHAPTER IX

IN SEARCH OF THE FINAL DOCTRINE

"There was never a good war or a bad peace".

—Benjamin Franklin

The best doctrine for asymmetric warfare is that there is 'no doctrine'. Each situation is uniquely fluid and calls for a fine blending of various factors which govern the relative advantage over the opponents. The dynamism of the situation depends upon the 'Human Terrain' in the conflict grid. It is not merely a 'war of guns' where conventional methodologies, largely based on GTM, could prove to be effective. Rather, neo-paradigms of the 'war of perceptions' generate a new spectrum of control where various stakeholders, governmental as well as insurgency augumented, constantly try to create their own foothold.

Factors Governing the Relative Advantage

The factors which govern the 'relative advantage' could

be many. Some of the vital vectors on such a grid appear to be as under:

- The accessibility of the government in terms of reach as well as the quality of governance in the core area.
- History of socio-political developments leaving various footprints of confluence, marginalization and particularizations in terms of religion, ethnic mix, linguistic profile, hold over natural resources and so on.
- The impact of economic and material development providing various types of vertical, horizontal and diagonal linkages, including the exchange of life style values. The hold of the private players.
- Effectiveness of socially mobilized 'community circles', their diversity and cohesiveness.
- Penetration of external influence groups by various means, tangible as well as intangible.
- Advent of technology in the life style, providing various options of sustenance, connectivity, networking and responses.
- Management of change in the core area in various critical fields, reformatory or otherwise, and the profile of catalysts trying to bring in the coveted changes.
- Homogeneity and heterogeneity in various segments of the core area formulating the matrix of relative deprivation amidst various oscillating expectations.
- Various stratifications in terms of the rich and the poor, rural and urban, literate and illiterate, elite and non elite, etc., which tend to create different pockets of anonymity, trust, equity and related risks.

Thus, in asymmetric warfare, in homeland problems, we deal with our own people where perceptions, propaganda, goodwill, trust and all such similar factors matter the most. The means of controlling disorder must meet the public approval. Public cooperation must flow voluntarily in favour of the governmental initiatives. The police and the public must become substitutive. The social response to 'security domains' must flow as an inbuilt feature. This is basically pertinent for two reasons. Firstly, society has enormous capacity to synergize through its various segments in the form of information flow, physical and material support, cognitive responses and counter propaganda. Secondly, the government agencies operate through people who have short tenures, limited stakes and superficial commitment. Then procedures become more important than the actual work in the government functioning while the lead response time ceases to be a priority.

Given the various complexities, one may lay stress on different derivatives and generate correlational profiles for the sake of conceptual understanding. However, it is enough here to say that each such conflict zone calls for an understanding based on a 'system analysis', and the 'SWOT' profiling as seen earlier. The Geographical and Human terrains, when analysed in terms of accessibility and visibility, would then generate both, sets of limiting as well as facilitating factors. One must take a critical view of them. Do not let anything be taken for granted. Accordingly, different response models will have to be evolved for the metropolitan, urban, semi urban, rural, forested and other categorized belts, clubbing geographical as well as the human terrain peculiarities, along with various influence systems operating at a given point of time.

Synergetic Response Modules

There are varying opinions as to the approach in tackling insurgencies. Some perceive them as purely security related problems and lay emphasis on capacity building within the security apparatus. While others view them as the outcome of developmental deficits and therefore focus on developmental domains. Since none of these approaches can work in isolation, further formats are conceived in terms of security linked development and vice versa. Each approach is exhaustive in its intrinsics. However, no exclusive or disjointed opinion can be given in favour of any of these approaches. Environmental dynamics entails various workable options of all such approaches, taken in different quantums, as per the need of the situation. Operational experience also shows that civic action programs clubbed with security operations have also paid rich dividends.

Security response model to various conflict situations in the Indian context has its base in the federal structure and the segmental initiatives. India is a union of states where law and order is the state subject. Hence, states have developed their own policing and internal security systems. Central government provides assistance to the states in terms of paramilitary forces, Central Police units and the fiscal resources for modernization, national investigation agency, forensic units, multi agency coordination centres and such similar initiatives that have been undertaken for better synergy and enhanced national level responses. Though various administrative ameliorations have been duly provided for, under the constitutional arrangements, the operational synthesis calls for neo formats. The problems are not local. Technologically exported global terror has made the role of central agencies more crucial. Various central agencies have, therefore, been integrated at the cutting edge level with the state security set up under the unified command system headed by the chief of the state government. Task forces and core groups have also been configured for catering to various operational requirements. Integration of security and developmental initiatives is also facilitated under such a system. Central government has also undertaken the initiatives to seal international borders with feasible access control systems. Indian model tends to underline the premises that democratic systems with decentralized empowerment can work better when compared to other options, given the diversities of religion, culture and civilization. These premises could be questioned as being a mere facade that provides a high opportunity cost with a lot of leverage being given to them under the democratic set up. However, democratic dispensations have been universally viewed as superior to the other dispensations the world over.

Customized Doctrine

Different countries are at different levels of development. They have their own strategic, political, social and economic particularizations. The degree of external linkages also differs as per the international reflection of their strategic and economic stakes. Different countries, therefore, have a different impact of possible conflicts and the resultant terror. They have devised their defence mechanism as per their own systemic intrinsics. The 'Homeland security' model of the US is one such example. For the sake of summarization, one can look into the selective security parameters which can be relevant to customize the security systems and develop a response mechanism for asymmetric warfare.

We should not take anything as given in the asymmetric warfare scenario having global linkages in the real as well as the virtual world. The technological advancements have made the conflict responses on either side very sophisticated. The NBC (Nuclear Biological and Chemical) options of well calibrated attacks entail altogether different counter responses and defence mechanisms. The information or cyber warfare is emerging as a new arena of espionage, infiltration, sabotage and subversion, more so in a situation where all the data bases, various transactions, control procedures, intelligence based smart security systems, infra-structural set ups and public services are thriving on the virtual networks.

All this leads us to conclude that our responses have to be 'well customized' for each situation. Thus, we should speak in terms of customized doctrines for each conflict situation which may have a finer mix of various relevant factors in different doses, as per their requirement. The 'relevant factors' have been depicted under various heads herein before. However, some of the most relevant factors can be reiterated for the sake of clarity and proper understanding:

- Surveillance and access control on various inroads into the area, to have a check on infiltration and exfiltrations.
- Developing data bank of insurgents, OGW support systems, frontal organizations and other networks. Identification of various conduits for infrastructural, operational and financial support.
- Level of technological adaptations and systemic integrations.
- Investigative trails and follow up action for neutralization, more as a pre-emptive action. A real victory without fighting the opponent. In asymmetric warfare, intelligent investigation and swift action can give enormous tactical advantage to weaken and liquidate the enemy.
- Community Policing formats, providing positive public interface and favourable responses.
- Perception management and psychological operations to channelize the public cognition in the right directions.

- Operational capacity building in terms of weaponary, equipments and logistics as well as the operational skills.
- Observance of Humane approach during operations.

CHAPTER X

NEO FORMATS OF TERRORISM

"The big thieves hang the little ones".

—Czech Proverb

The well calibrated terror tactics have become the usual feature of asymmetric warfare. As such, the need for innovative modus operandi remains high on the agenda of the adversaries. The neo life style formats and the developmental initiatives in public arenas are, therefore, exploited to the point of destruction. This point shall become amply clear if we consider some of the formats that are crucial.

There have been tremendous advancements in the field of mobility and navigation. These options are exploited to act as courier of terrorism. To start with, land transport has been vastly exploited to create widespread terror and a deep sense of insecurity. Vehicles have been used not only for concealed transportation of arms and explosives but also for initiating explosions of various types. Vehicles also provide the advantage of a secondary explosion that is caused by its fuel.

Similarly, serial train blasts, including the use of incendiary bombs, have been resorted to in order to generate a strong perception of terror and for effectively impacting and shaking the public confidence.

Examples of aviation terrorism are also vastly available across the globe. Hijacking (hostage) as well as a threat of blowing up of aircrafts are terror tactics used to force the governments to concede to the demands of the terrorists. The flying machine with the potential for a high degree explosion has also been used as a 'bomb'. Now-a-days, threats also loom large with the private aircrafts, helicopters, micro light machines, gliders, etc., being used for various purposes, including adventure sports, whose use could be exploited by terror designers.

It will be a serious aberration if we ignore the exploitative use of the maritime zones. The stories of sea pirates have to be rewritten in a different context. Besides concealed transportation of IEDs, explosives, arms and ammunitions through commercial shipping avenues, various 'choke points' have been used as an opportunity to delay essential supplies, including the inputs used in the energy sector. Oil expels have been used to generate vast devastations, physically, economically as well as environmentally. Uninhabited islands have been used as safe sanctuaries. It is difficult to monitor the infiltration and subversion in the human settlements around the coastal areas.

Energy security is an important aspect in modern life where all our sustenance depends on the uninterrupted supply of fuel and power. One of the easiest ways to get everything to a standstill is to sabotage the energy sector.

Communication security constitutes yet another area of modern life which needs to be sustained against any debacle or mishap. It encompasses all types of commonly known communication systems such as HF/VHF/CDMA/GSM/ IP/ V-SAT.

In fact the 'war of perceptions' and 'communication terrorism' are deeply related. The PSYWAR through internet sites, blogs, chat rooms, mails is more potent than the other options. Cyber terrorism promotes sabotage and infiltration of the virtual world on the net, where all the transactions of real life are substituted in digital formats and networked across the globe. Data destruction remains a major domain of net-centric terrorism. Programmes could be devised and used to trigger various upheavals where network systems are being used to control critical activities.

Last, but not the least, information warfare may also take an ugly turn.

CHAPTER XI

POLITICAL GOVERNANCE AND TERRORISM

"Politics is war without bloodshed while war is politics with bloodshed".

—Mao Zedong

The quality of the political governance is the key to public management. The occurrence of a political vacuum, or the lack of good governance, leaves the society in a frictional state. The cohesiveness required to sustain the public sanctity evaporates. The disintegrative forces then mutate fast to grant cavity to the players in the art of terrorism.

The quality of political governance is often determined by the equality of opportunities granted by the system to individuals for their self actualized sustenance, devoid of any discrimination. It purports to cleanse all the patches of corruption which eclipse the integrity and transparency of the system. It, inter-alia, means wiping out all the plausible causes of anger in the public, or at least, opening the doors of justice, reconciliation and dialogue for a conducive environment towards conflict resolution.

It is said that good policies help in clearing the terror nurseries, and good legal governance neutralizes the culprits. Prima facie, there cannot be two opinions on it. However, policies have to be differentiated from excessive promulgation of law as a substitute for social change. Most of the vectors on the conflict grid may have their eruptions not through the ideological fault lines, as is commonly perceived, but through the managerial mess created by faulty political governance.

Time and again the political approach to tackle conflicts has been regarded as the best possible option in the vicious loop of 'public management'. The bureaucratic set up provides a temporary interface between the officers and the local populace. The temporary induction of outside security forces may manage to get a feel of the geographical terrain, but cannot really get the required insights into the human terrain. The 'blind self' situation leads to a series of apprehensions and misguided responses. The hostilities further marginalize the sanctity of any confidence building measures which could otherwise be used to patch up the rifts. The line of difference between the best and the worst is very thin. Viewed from the other side, the political mismanagement has been found to be the prime factor in boosting terrorism. In fact, when the civilized form of public representation fails to deliver results through well institutionalized systems then the power of the gun, justified on grounds of well bracketed ideologies, finds its way to fill up the vacuum. In either case the 'public' remains the point of control as well as the point of sustenance.

The political management of counter insurgency apparatus is also one of the critical domains. The cost benefit matrix of the varying options of using brutal force for neutralizing the terror modules, more so in a civic environment, provides a scenario quite akin to the chemotherapy procedures employed to counter a fast spreading cancer. It may not necessarily be a well targeted therapy to neutralize the cancerous cells hence a combination of various immunity building therapies could provide comparatively better solutions.

Innovative management is, therefore, the key to success. Environmental scanning and conducive management tactics could facilitate the neutralization of terror modules present there. The varying combinations of security linked development, and vice-versa, then become dominant in decision making.

In societies that are not well developed, stratifications give rise to mutually disjointed public sub-groups, each thriving on their own sub-culture. The cavities of terror intervention become quite distinct and facilitating. The developed societies too nurture terrorism, but in a different context. Their contents may also differ. There could be different levels of game play. Though the game may not be apparently so lucrative, yet, the power games that evolve have their own intricacies.

At this juncture, it is sufficient to grasp the basics of 'power domains' in managing the public. The formats and the processes here may differ. The political governance and terrorism, cetrus paribus, could be mutually competitive.

Chapter XII

Global and Neighbourhood Linkages

"Terrorism has become the systematic weapon of war that knows no borders or seldom has a face".

—Jacques Chirac

The conflicts on the internal security grid may no longer remain only a localised phenomenon for various reasons. Rather, they may acquire different shades:

- The players in a long drawn conflict situation may look for external help in terms of funds, supply of arms and other support options.
- Uncordial neighbours may grant shelter, training base and various kinds of accessibilities to the adversary.
- The infiltration of 'hardware as well as software' for the perpetuation of a well calibrated violence level, to suit the strategic and diplomatic stakes in the neighborhood as well as at the global level.

- The creation and sustenance of support groups for psychological warfare, which is a more potent weapon than direct onslaught.
- The nurturing of 'local sleeper cells' which could be activated at an opportune moment.

The strategic linkages across the globe may even result in various permutations and combinations. Big players at the global level try to placate the smaller nations in order to enhance their area of dominance and influence. The diplomatic strokes are configured accordingly.

Today, the need for economic dominance has captured the attention of the political players. The nuclear deterrence, emergence of global and regional bodies to watch strategic interests and the 'game of perceptions' have shifted the focus away from the brutal formats of supremacy. The highly monitored market forces now rule the roost.

Interestingly, the technological advancement has also helped in exporting terror. The information dissemination in terms of its volume, integrity and real time processing has added new domains. The remote controlled characteristic of asymmetric warfare now makes it more challenging to capture the adversaries. The virtual warfare has gradually replaced the real battlefield.

Last, but not the least, the international goodwill in the wake of gross awareness across civilized societies, for peaceful co-existence, has forced the power players to refine their diplomatic moves. The dichotomy between the 'normative ' and the 'coveted' gives rise to ulterior strokes in fanning the invisible and the intangible terror. It is not necessary that the tangible occurrence of such 'honey-quoted' terror moves is deciphered to arrive at the truth. The propagated truth always eludes reality.

Having theorized upon the empirical observations, it is now not very difficult to appreciate why a duck may not always appear to be a duck. It is not difficult to understand why intelligence agencies still look for the 'duck'. We may refrain from further mystical elaborations if we can correlate the trans-territorial phenomenon with the eruptions on the internal security grid.

The asymmetric warfare may have a remote trigger. Merely curing local symptoms may not help in eradicating the problem. This also explains why the experts choose to write what they themselves would not like to adhere to.

Following excerpts in the Indian context are quoted in support of the premises drawn herein above:

> A: "After the independence of India, and the accompanying division of the subcontinent, the countries in the region have been at war with one another. However, apart from a few 'limited' or comparatively short-scale wars, the conflicts have been 'proxy wars', namely the sponsorship of insurgencies and terrorist groups in order to bleed, pester and humiliate one another. Providing insurgents or terrorists of an enemy country with a safe haven, arms, training, and the like, is a phenomenon that is embedded in the post-colonial state policy and diplomacy of South Asia.
>
> Therefore, even as Pakistan continues to support the terrorists groups in Kashmir, it is Bangladesh that has become the most important 'bureau' of Pakistan's Inter Services Intelligence (ISI) in the region. It is from its erstwhile eastern wing that Pakistan launches their covert operations in the Indian mainland and North East India. Pakistan's sustenance and aid to the insurrection in Kashmir has already been documented. It would suffice, therefore, to inform further that Pakistan has 'activated' a second front against Kashmir, from Bangladesh, in order to pin down the Indian security forces in North East India from being deployed in Kashmir. Also, the violence that has erupted in India, particularly after 9/11 has indisputably proven the hands of the Islamist groups of

both Pakistan and Bangladesh, with active support from their respective intelligence agencies. This has become evident from the confessional statements of apprehended and surrendered Islamist cadres in Assam.

It is indeed a fact that in the case of South Asia, countries have attempted to settle scores by taking advantage of the insurgencies in rival countries. The distinctive aspect that characterizes this phenomenon is the response that the nation-states provide. The region's geopolitics is defined to a considerable extent by the reciprocal patronage of insurgencies over a sustained period of time, as, was the case when India supported East Pakistan's freedom fighters, by embarking on a full-scale military intervention. Only countries such as Sri Lanka, Bhutan, Maldives, and Nepal have more or less refrained from entering into the games of 'proxy war'. But, the other countries of the region, namely Pakistan, China (a key factor in South Asia), India, and Bangladesh have almost perfected this into a near-acceptable form of offensive diplomacy. Therefore, if Pakistan aids the global Salafi movement in Kashmir, India had supported the "Mukti Bahini' (freedom fighters) in Bangladesh, ensuring primarily that a hostile Pakistan is rid of an eastern flank. Also, if India backed the Amdo and the Khampa insurgents against the Chinese occupation of Tibet in the past, the Chinese responded by aiding the North East Indian insurgent organizations. If Islamabad backed the Khalistan groups in Punjab, and later organizations such as the National Socialist Council of Nagalim (NSCN) and the ULFA, New Delhi reportedly backed the Mohajir outfits in Pakistan's Sind province. Indeed, even the unrest that had gripped China's Tibet Autonomous Region during the run-up to the Beijing Olympics in March 2008 might have been facilitated by a 'look-the-other-way' option followed by India, even as it allowed the United States to embrace Beijing during a crucial period for China. It is also possible that New Delhi seized an opportunity and, thereby, embarked on such a course of action because it wanted to send a message to Beijing to stop making statements that pertained to its purported claim over India's Arunachal Pradesh. It is such an action that illustrates the ways in which 'proxy wars' are waged in South Asia. The 'strategic encirclement' of North East India and the attendant problem of New Delhi's insensitivity has made the region into a veritable 'proxy war' playfield".

(Circle of design, Jaideep Saikia; *Terrorism, Patterns of Internalization*; Sage publications, New Delhi, 2009)

The internal radicalization and indoctrination of the 'mind set' on a set of given vectors, beyond the realm of well demarcated geographical boundaries or emotionally nurtured national domains, have given rise to new contours on the spectrum of global terrorism.

B: "Part of the problem is the fact that the overall rise in the lethality of terrorist violence is not a two dimensional proposition along the religious vs secular divide, but is also influenced by many additional dynamic factors, most importantly, the growing level of internationalization of terrorist networks and the process of 'democratization of a destructive power'. Due mainly to the rapid proliferation of advanced technologies, the presence of a large, well-funded, and highly organized group is no longer a precondition to the occurrence of destructive terrorists plots, as even small groups of individuals are increasingly gaining the capacity to inflict considerable damage. Especially influential in this regard has been the boom of the Internet, which has become instrumental in significantly aiding the efficiency of terrorist operations. This has included the facilitation of easy access to astonishing quantities of instructional material that theoretically enable the terrorists to acquire useful skills, such as knowledge on how to manufacture explosives and potent poisons from dual-use materials, or the technical specifications of buildings, power plants, and other potential targets. Information technologies have also aided the ' new terrorists' in studying their enemies' investigative capabilities and operational procedures, thus providing the aptitude to further identify and exploit potential weaknesses and vulnerabilities. As a result, even small groups of terrorists with limited resources are now arguably gaining the capacity to organize increasingly sophisticated operations".

(*Transnational Terrorism*, Adam Dolnik; Ibid)

CHAPTER XIII

RELEVANCE OF POLICING IN TERROR CONTAINMENT

"Action cures fear, inaction creates terror".

The militaristic approach is not fully relevant in an asymmetric warfare environment. The enemy is not across the well defined geographical borders, but unobtrusively mingled with the local populace. He derives covert as well as overt support from the local habitat. Psychological dominance grants him a leverage to manipulate public response in his favour and, more often than not, he uses the local political clout as well as the criminal networking.

Under such an environment, the investigation tools acquire greater importance in unearthing the terror network and the modules operating there at. The terror trail, once identified and traced in terms of its locus, can be mitigated to neutralize the support systems of the adversary.

Policing approach would also help in locating and targeting the top leaders in the opponent's hierarchy. The human rights activism getting stronger, the need for evidence collection is of crucial importance in order to pursue the necessary process of law. With the changing life styles and technologies, one has to observe the well defined codes of the social as well as legal apparatus. It is in this context that the civil police component has to merge well with the paramilitary set up, modified to suit the asymmetric warfare environment. And in order not to undermine the importance of the local human terrain, the civil police set up can be optimally used to provide a strong interface, much desired in such situations, to facilitate the effectiveness of the outside forces inducted into the area for various armed interventions. This is similar to the role of a general healthcare expert who determines the nature, timing, duration and extent of surgical intervention on a case to case basis.

In an asymmetric warfare environment on the internal security grid, the need for security based development calls for a strong participative response from all agencies where the local police can successfully provide a strong interface. Effective policing would also tend to evolve guidelines for all the governmental as well as non-governmental agencies which could help in choking the conduits used by the adversary in nurturing its own systems.

The socio-economic set up uses the given resources to maximize the utility of various products and services. The resources available for social sustenance could be used by the opponent in creating a means of mass destruction. Chemicals meant for fertilizers, medicines and other purposes are used to create explosives. The resources used in the mining industry have also been diverted on the terror grid. The new technologies in telecom sector have been misused to develop remote explosions. Under such a situation, the need for an agency to track down such misuses and mitigate the adverse impacts cannot be undermined. Once again, the onus falls on the civil police to deliver the expected results.

CHAPTER XIV

CRISIS MANAGEMENT PLANS FOR TERROR ATTACKS

"Fighting terrorism is like being a goalkeeper. You can make a hundred brilliant saves but the only shot that people remember is the one that gets past you".

—Paul Wilkinston

It would be prudent to glance through the outlines of a crisis management plan which could be put in place to counter the terror attacks. In fact, a sequence of actions to be taken by various agencies, along with the standard operating procedures for each action could be essential ingredients of such a plan. A planned approach provides better chances of effective action, rather than incoherent 'escape – avoidance' response in times of crisis.

The important steps could be as under:

- Formation of well structured Crisis Management Groups (CMGs) and the emergency response centres at the national, federal and district level, integrating various departments and agencies with their clearly defined responses and responsibilities. The emergency response centres should be configured to assimilate all the required data for decision support systems (DSS) and customized to receive, process and coordinate the operational disseminations. It would be a good practice to specify some alternate members. Dissemination of the information to public and the media should also receive due priority, hence the CMGs should invariably provide for such an interface. Precise, cogent and real time communications are of critical importance in such emergencies.

- A hub of well configured, suitably trained, sufficiently equipped and highly committed search and rescue teams, along with tactical capabilities, be created keeping in view the congruency of the geographical and human terrain.
- Expert groups to handle negotiations, in case of a hostage situation, could be formulated in advance with sufficient data bank and DSS network.
- Intelligence network for actionable operational-inputs must be in place.
- Role and response levels of various types of forces, at different phases of emergency, need to be defined to avoid duality of command and control.
- Damage control exercises must also be provided for.

In fact, vulnerability and risk assessment ought to be a constant exercise in order to change over from a 'response-centric' approach to the 'proactive' and 'holistic' modules. The level of preparedness and mitigation programmes can be accordingly upgraded. GIS platforms with multilayered data integration, as per vulnerability mapping, could be a wonderful DSS tool for various stakeholders.

Peace time capacity building, mock drills, simulations, feedback based refinements in SOPs are some of the factors which would affect the quality of responses in case of emergency. Another factor is the placement of competent coordinators in CMG and key catalysts in various operational agencies.

In an era of technologically integrated global terrorism, the control points of 'terror-triggers' could be well beyond the national jurisdiction. Hence, the role of external agencies in all spheres, primarily policing, intelligence as well as diplomacy could be of greater significance in international cooperation in order to mitigate the given threats.

data integration, as per vulnerability mapping, could be a wonderful DSS tool for various stakeholders.

Peace time capacity building, mock drills, simulations, feedback based refinements in SOPs are some of the factors which would affect the quality of responses in case of emergency. Another factor is the placement of competent coordinators in CMG and key catalysts in various operational agencies.

In an era of technologically integrated global terrorism the control points of terror triggers could be well beyond the national jurisdiction. Hence, the role of external agencies in all spheres, primarily policing, intelligence as well as diplomacy could be of greater significance for international cooperation in order to mitigate the given threats.

CHAPTER XV

MEDIA NORMS AND TERRORISM

"We must try to find ways to starve the terrorist and the hijacker of the oxygen of publicity on which they depend".

—Margaret Thatcher

It is the responsibility of the media to provide factually correct information that is objective in nature. However, it should be configured and designed appropriately so as not to propagate:

- anything that hurts the sentiments of any particular community.
- anything that facilitates publicity or glamorizes the terrorist or their ideologies or evokes sympathy.
- anything that enhances the risks to the captives of a situation.
- anything that fans violence or mutual hatred.

- anything that covers operational details which may hamper the success or the impact of the operations.
- anything that shakes public confidence.

The line of difference between the normative and factual responses of the media could subsist where it may be difficult to really demarcate the faultlines. However, a single window of information flow, with real time reliable dissemination, could be adopted by the authorities in order to avoid confusion and divergent views created by a plethora of official agencies in the fray.

Hence, it is imperative to have a media policy and a good media management system. Media facilitation platforms could be provided where authorized spokespersons should be ready with all the details 24 x 7, keeping in touch with all the functionaries during crisis management. This system needs to be established at different levels - national, federal as well as district.

Necessary code of conduct could be put in place with a monitory mechanism. To cite an example, Cable Television Network Rules 1994 in India provides for such codes. Necessary prohibitions have been defined. No programme can be telecast which:

- Offends decency
- Contains criticism of friendly Countries
- Condemns religious or ethnic groups or has tendency to incite violence
- Denigrates women, children or other vulnerable segments
- Contains aspersions against the country or the sovereign heads or the judiciary, etc.
- Airs anything which is unsuitable for unrestricted exhibition or prohibited otherwise as an open social code or public conduct.

The regulatory mechanism provides for the creation of state and district level monitoring committees. Authorized officers are designated to initiate the monitoring mechanism. Such a system provides for an interface between the public and the state as well as the media and helps the state in finding congruent levels of media dispositions.

Rectificationary measures could include anything from an advisory to the tendering of an apology and the suspension of broadcasts.

In practice, however, it is really difficult to arrive at a system which can be foolproof. It is, at times, really difficult to delineate objectivity from the rest. It is not feasible to find the acceptable level of optima with respect to various prohibitions. The perceptional incongruence may not be so easily deciphered on the spot, before much avoidable damage takes place. The legalities may be subject to divergent interpretations.

Hence, the best way is to evolve a strong professional code of conduct and a healthy public audit mechanism. A balance has to be found between the freedom of press for proper public information and the larger public good.

CHAPTER XVI

ETHICS IN COUNTER INSURGENCY RESPONSES

"In time of war the first casualty is truth".

—Booke Carter

The question of ethics in counter insurgency responses has been much debated. In fact, when we speak of the state sponsored violence induced to counter insurgency and terrorism, the onus of observing optimum rationalities while using 'force' falls on the state authorities with a wide range of protocols and public scanners:

- Minimum possible use of force for minimum desirable period.
- Fundamental rights to be observed in favour of the perpetrator of violence.
- Custodial norms, avoidance of torture and cruelty.
- Right to cause death, subject to self defence norms and adequate warning.

The various codes in this context are well enumerated in the national and international Conventions. The human rights domains have also been well demarcated over a period of time.

The realm of ethics goes much beyond this. It may start with the confidence building measures, surrender and rehabilitation packages in order to get the disgruntled and misguided elements back into the national main stream and extend to the resettlement of widows and orphans of militancy. These may still be regarded as the extrinsics of the ethical contours. The intrinsic platforms have to be built around the non lethal neutralization of the insurgents, compassionate behavioural nurturing and unfreezing of the indoctrinated learning that triggers extreme protest behaviour. It may sound quite inappropriate to a soldier or a cop who is endangering his life while deployed on the counter emergency grid. However, the bottom line remains that the code of state sponsored violence has to be distinctly different than those of the insurgency sponsored violence, both in its context as well as content.

All wars end in peace. There cannot be endless circles of hate and violence. However, it may take time. The impact of the violence based responses may leave sharper marks in the short run, than the long term demonstration effect of the ethical norms that would tend to have a greater stability and resilience. This may, however, remain as a premise till the historical events are once again unearthed to substantiate it.

CHAPTER XVII

RECENT TRENDS IN USE OF EXPLOSIVES IN TERROR ATTACKS

"You can't say civilization is not advancing, in every war they kill you in a new way".

—Anonymous

Improvised explosive devices (IED) have been frequently used with various types of triggering mechanism, detonators and explosive substances. The IED may take any shape of a commonly used item in a given environment. The mechanism for initializing or activating any detonation could be either mechanical, electrical, chemical, radio controlled, cellular, PIR or of other spectrums. The plausible permutation and combinations in each of these fields are constantly growing with the inception of new technologies. Different intensities could deliver different results. The timing of triggering such a mechanism is also now very accurate and precise. Actions can be controlled from a remote point. Such formats are often enabled to facilitate varied digital combinations, along with the micro controlled IC based circuits.

Over a period of time, there has been a comparative shift from high explosives, such as RDX, TNT, PETN, SEMTEX [RDX +PETN], to the commercially used explosives. Different choices of nitrate explosives, peroxide explosives and commercial explosives are available to create a blast. Various types of incendiaries and improvised explosive can be tabulated as under:

FUEL		
Fuel	**Colour / Flame**	**Use**
Acetone	Colourless liquid solvent	Most commonly used to prepare compound - Triacetone Triperoxide in combination with hydrogen peroxide.
Aluminium powder	Silver grey metal powder	Increases heat in mixtures.
Ammonia	Colourless liquid	Forms explosive compounds with Iodine, Mercury or Chlorine.
Charcoal	Black powder or chunks of burnt wood	Mixing with Potassium Nitrate+ Sulphur (Gunpowder).

Gasoline	Clear yellow liquid	Inflammable Substance: Molotov- Gasoline +K oil (Kerosene); Gasoline +CaC2+ Diesel; Gasoline +K oil+ H2So4 .
Glycerine	Clear thick liquid	Produces hypergolic reaction with - Calcium hydrochloride, Potassium permanganate.
Magnesium powder	Silver metal powder	Hypergolic characteristics/ Improve brilliance of firework
Metallic sodium	Soft silver like metal.	Turns grey if exposed in air. Ignites when in contact with water

Red Phosphorous	Red to violet crystals Red	Phosphorous forms sensitive explosive mixtures with metal halogenates (e.g., Chlorates or Bromate of Barium M, Calcium, Magnesium, Potassium, Sodium, or Zinc), Ammonium Nitrate, Silver Nitrate, Sodium Nitrate, and Potassium Permanganate
Sugar	White granular powder	Enhances combustion With $KClO_3$ +Sulphur
Vaseline	White waxy material	$KClO_3$ +Vaseline (called poor man's C4)
Sulphur	Pale yellow powder	Makes mixtures more sensitive

Table - 12

OXIDIZERS		
Oxidizers	**Colour / Flame**	**Use**
Ammonium Nitrate	White pills / powder	Used in making ANFO.
Calcium Hypochlorite	Yellow white solid	Ignites in contact with organic materials.
Ferric Oxide	Reddish brown	Relatively non-reactive oxidizer.
Hexamine	White crystalline material	Used to manufacture HMTD
Hydrogen Peroxide	Looks like water	Used to manufacture TATP.
Iodine crystal	Dark blue crystals	Reacts with water causing combustion with fuels.
Potassium Chlorate	White granules	Hypergolic reaction with Sulphuric acid.
Potassium Chloride	White granules	Explosive reaction with organic fuels.
Potassium Nitrate	White crystals	Make black powder.
Potassium Chlorate	White granules	Produce extremely sensitive mixture with Red Phosphorus.

Potassium Permanganate	Dark purple crystals	Hypergolic reaction with Glycerin, Sulphuric acid ; Explosive mixture with Red Phosphorus.
Sulphuric acid	Colourless, slightly oily liquid	Hypergolic reaction with: Black powder, Potassium Chlorate, Sodium peroxide, Calcium hyper chlorate; Explosive reaction with Potassium Permanganate.

Table - 13

Incendiaries

(a) Potassium Chlorate (or) Sodium Chlorate + Powder sugar: Ignited by Sulphuric Acid.

(b) Plaster of Paris (POP) + Aluminium powder: Ignited by Sulphuric acid.

(c) Potassium Nitrate +Red Phosphorus: Ignited by Sulphuric acid.

(d) Iodine Crystal + Aluminium Powder: Ignited by water.

(e) Metallic Sodium: Ignited by water.

(f) Potassium Permanganate + Powder sugar: Ignited by Glycerin.

(g) Sodium Peroxide + Sugar: Ignited by Gasoline.

Common Improvised Explosives

Improvised explosives are made from a mixture of commonly used chemicals available in the market for industrial or agricultural use:

(a) Gun powder + Potassium Nitrate

(b) Fire Cracker Material

(c) Potassium Nitrate + Aluminium powder +Sulphur

(d) Potassium Nitrate + Sugar

(e) Barium Nitrate + Aluminium Powder +Sulphur

(f) NFO + Ammonium Nitrate + Fuel oil

(g) POP + Magnesium

(h) Ammonium Nitrate + Naphthalene balls +Potassium Chlorate

(i) Ammonium Nitrate + Aluminum Powder + Potassium Chloride +Charcoal

(j) Ammonium Nitrate + Aluminum Powder

(k) Calcium Nitrate + Aluminum Powder

(l) Picric Acid + Aspirin Tablets + Alcohol

Easy availability, portability, low price, easy use, difficulty in identifying the source, no leftover evidence are some of the facilitative features for the terror elements using these options.

Any discussion on explosives would be incomplete unless we speak of the more fatal forms of explosions than the common IEDs. This brings us to the use of car bombs and human bombs. Analysis of such incidents in India have shown the following usage:

- RDX or high grade commercial explosives.
- Radio controlled triggering mechanism, 3-5 DTMF (Rx) codes with VHF receivers (TX)
- Subsidiary blasts in car bombs through gas cylinders and the fuel tanks.
- Mobile phones with micro chips - RCIED.

Scientific exploitation is a game of wit. One may keep trying to the point of self subversion.

Liquid bombs add a new dimension. By using various refined chemicals, which may give the appearance of commonly used liquid items, various combinations are generated to enable well timed and well intensified blasts.

During recent times, non nitrogen explosives like triacetone triperoxide (TATP) and hexamethylene triperoxidediamine (HMTD) have become explosives of choice used by the terror groups, besides ANFO, TOVEX or EMULEX, etc.

CBRNE is another zone of concern. Chemical, Biological, Radiological, Nuclear Explosive could be used with dispersal devices in several manners, e.g., dispersion of radioactive aerosols; detonating such material with conventional explosives (dirty bomb), etc.

The journey of explosions and blasts from pressure and claymore mines to various types of IEDs is seemingly endless. The counter IED efforts are accordingly being intensified with varying degrees of success. We may enlist a few of them:

- Dogs, rats, bees
- Trace excessive detection
- Chemical Identification Kit
- Electron Capture Detection

- Chemiluminescence
- Thermo -redox
- Iron Mobility Spectrometry
- Field Iron Spectrometry
- Photoluminescence
- Resonance enhanced multi-photo ionization
- Laser induced spectroscopy/ Laser imaging /Laser induced fluorescence
- X-ray techniques
- Nuclear techniques - Thermal Neutron Activation (TNA), Pulsed Fast Neutron Activation (PFNA), and neutron based pulsed elemental analysis.

CHAPTER XVIII

TECHNOLOGY AS FORCE MULTIPLIER

"The risk with technology is that it is self- subversive".

—MK Narayanan

The profile of technological upgradations for operational purposes can be briefly categorized, as under, for the sake of clarity as well as functionality:

- Proactive gears
- Detective and disposal equipments
- Area and object scanning gadgets
- Area navigation aids
- Mobility - speed, security and terrain specific features
- Communication devices
- Precision firing attachment

- Multilayered GIS platforms
- Multipurpose integrative modules

Undoubtedly, technologies provide effective options to enhance operational efficiency and cut down on human intervention, however, one has to be watchful of the following factors:

a) They have to be customized for specific use with given cost benefit implications.

b) The obsolescence is very high.

c) The technology is self subversive; the opponents can neutralize it using counter methods.

There is a wider range of options in each category. Market forces have generated enough competition to deliver quality products based on the user requirements. The global networking has facilitated the place and time utility for such products. While safety, weight, ergonomic suitability and other such factors have become critical, the intelligence based smart technologies are available for a proactive response. However, it is to be done with caution against any type of intrusion, interference or improvisation. A wide spectrum of electro-magnetic waves has been manipulated to support these plans. Even in the field of navigation and communication various bandwidths have been used, augmented by transmission aids. It could be a repeater, a tower or the geo-station linked satellite. Some of the examples can be cited as under:

- GIS solutions: for operational planning
- Anti-Fragmentation Vest: for self protection
- Smart Fence: for perimeter security
- Smart and Intelligent Camera Systems: for visual scanning and detection
- Rapid Wire System: for fencing

- Wire Locator: to detect buried command wires
- Optical Fibro scope: to view cavities
- Disrupter and Water Cannon: to break circuit of IED from a safe distance
- Total Containment Vessel: to transport and dispose off explosive devices
- Remote Operating Vehicle: for remote handling of explosive devices
- Real time viewing system: viewing suspected devices for confirmation of IED
- Backpack UAV: for aerial photography/surveillance of area
- LSP Ranger: for day/night 360° surveillance
- Stalker Vehicle: for high accuracy 'target acquisition' and 'auto tracking'
- Portable X-ray: to view internal contents of any packed or sealed item
- Wall Radar: highlights moving objects
- Vehicle Scanner: for complete scanning of vehicle
- Under Vehicle Scanner : to scan underneath the vehicle
- Eye Ball: used for 360° scanning
- Day / Night Vision device & Binoculars: for strain free night vision, surveillance and reconnaissance
- Thermal Imager: to get clear thermal image in complete darkness
- Infrared Sensor: to see the object in darkness without getting exposed
- Armored Vehicle: to provide defence against sharpnels and ambushes

- RCIED Jammer: to secure against remote controlled IEDs by blocking the signals
- GPS: to provide reliable time information & location
- Satellite Telephone: to facilitate communication anywhere through satellite
- Corner Shot with upgraded assault rifle: useful for room intervention
- Infrared Laser Pointer: for accurate marking of target and covert illumination
- Mini Reflex Sight: for aimed fire through hologram from various positions
- Explorer: multi function command and control observation system; binocular integrated with GPS, real time data transfer, co-ordinates and range finder facilities
- Soldier Communication System: a hands free operation, radio set, GPS compatibility
- LSMR Mobile Range: a customized firing range on a mobile van
- Technical surveillance: it includes:
    - Loggers/Digital recorders/ Mobile phones with GPS tracking
    - Cyber monitoring software
    - Audio bugging devices
    - Cyber forensic tools

CHAPTER XIX

CUSTOMIZED TRAINING MODULES

"Imagination is more important than knowledge".

—Albert Einstein

Human Resource Development is the core area for any organization. Man behind the show is always important, more so in the asymmetric war situations, where operational tactics and human terrain management are of crucial importance. In fact, following essentials can be cited as the minimum success factors:

i. Capability to make appropriate operational assessment.

ii. Operational capabilities for:

- Urban warfare scenario
- Jungle warfare
- Source handling
- Crisis management

iii. Positive leadership influence

iv. Insights into group dynamics and team building

v. Adaptability to emerging technologies

vi. Risk bearing aptitude, error tolerance

A proper training-need analysis may be conducted to assess the response capacity deficit. It is equally imperative to appreciate this fact that operational responses need to be modified as per the typicality of the local geographical and human terrain, given the modus operandi of the adversary. Further, the quality of the human resource and the conduciveness of the learning environment are also crucial vectors. Hence, one may choose to imbibe the basics from a similar training environment. Nevertheless, the need for proper customization cannot be undermined with respect to the 'specifics' in a given situation.

Learning by doing through proper demonstration effect in a well simulated environment could be far more effective than the traditional lecture oriented transmission skills. Looking into the varied dimensions of technology based operational responses, the option of outsourcing the training to experts having a core competence has become the need of the day. In other words, the training domains have also undergone intrinsic changes such that collaborative open systems of learning are far more effective than organizationally perceived stereotype modules. The networking culture, thus, offers more potent solutions.

Once regarded as the 'dumping ground', the training domains are now regarded as the most dynamic and potent segments. The organizations not responsive to this paradigm shift are bound to degrade. R&D in the field of 'learning' and seeking appropriate behavioural as well as operational responses has now become the top priority of strategic commanders on the combat grid. A new dimension of 'motivational learning' and 'conducive training environment' has been receiving a comparatively higher focus.

Important learning areas as on date can be cited as follows:

1. Jungle warfare
2. Urban warfare
3. Security
4. Intelligence generation
5. Explosives
6. Human Terrain management
7. Psychological operations
8. Perception management
9. Technological adaptations
10. Investigation and detection
11. Forensic technology
12. Cyber crime
13. Computer forensics
14. Communications
15. Technological surveillance
16. Money laundering
17. Community policing
18. Riot Control - use of non lethal means
19. Leadership command and control
20. Modernisation
21. Media handling
22. Group dynamics and behavioural responses
23. Healthcare and fitness
24. Motivation and welfare
25. Managing synergies

Chapter XX

Recapitulation

"It's more fun to arrive at a conclusion than to justify it".

—Malcolm Forbes

Counter insurgency strategies, as we learn, hover around oscillating vectors calling for a unique customized response each time. Arriving at any equilibrium, across various sub optima, involves a long and painful process. Insurgencies have been used as a tool for political change. However, the modus operandi has undergone a tremendous change with technology, global linkages and emergence of non state players. 'Cultural war' based on ideologies and a struggle for self determination has added further complexities. War amongst people, as against the conventional war between entities forms a new trend. The infrastructure required for such type of conflicts, akin to proxy wars, has also been reconfigured. The 'safe haven' enablers are also well within the logistical networks. Starting with persuasion, the process may involve anything from coercion to intimidation and use of blatant violence. The growth of a virtual world across the cyber space has completely changed the battlefields. The war of information and cyber terrorism present an unbound zone of conflict.

It is, therefore, essential to understand the nature of conflict and define the 'intent' with which we are customising our responses. 'People' are at the crux of the 'conflict'. The success would largely depend upon which way the people move. Hence, it is imperative to communicate with the people, attending to their legitimate grievances within the overall gamut of security. It has to be a people centric approach. However, it would be wise to remember that most people tend to flow along the current, as does the fish. What we need is to identify the direction and the force of the current and the game plans of the players.

In so far as the people are concerned, they need a secure environment. The issue of preventive security remains crucial and promotes stability. Preventive security may range from perimeter guarding target hardening, access control to intelligent surveillance, tracking systems to forensic analysis, so on and so forth.

Along with the preventive security, investigative and detective methodologies need to be appropriately pursued. One must also give due importance to the war of perception which now sets the direction of the current. Given the level of consciousness amidst real time connectivity and the dominance of the virtual world over the physical configurations, one has to face increasing constraints while navigating through conflict zones. The 'freedom slots' would be often nonexistent. It would be a battle of information, where accuracy and timing would determine the outcome.

Victory would largely hinge upon appropriate indigenous resources. Though the local geography matters, but now the precedence would have to be given to the human terrain. A visible symbol of 'moral justification' would have to be evolved through a set of flexible rules based on equity and equitability. The rule of law has to be felt and experienced, and not merely confined to books.

It is of no use to fight a war which one cannot win. Hence particularities of a war situation have to be well understood in order to customize the response. This is our basic premise which needs to be recalled again and again in order to remind us that what we need is the capability to be innovative every moment. Value of information, adaptability and flexibility has to be well understood and often revisited. It is important to work with an open mind and keep redefining the rules of engagement. A minimum use of force with fair means, through 'culturally aware indigenous forces' tends to prove to be better and more effective in a situation of 'war amongst people'. War of perception calls for the winning of the minds and the hearts of the local populace. This entails a synergetic response from multiple agencies, security as well as developmental. Neutralization of insurgents through mortal liquidation could be a farcical exercise, when in vain. Hence, success stories in handling insurgencies find their genesis in civilian control. That means that a police response in place of militaristic solution would be more desirable. Civic responses offer superior solution domains. Even when global network of insurgency finds its way through a marriage of convenience, it can be effectively neutralized through open collaborative formats in a multi agency environment. Here the opponent has to be beaten at his own game.

The continuum of primitive to advanced habitats may present varied life styles along with differential cognitive vectors. However, the basics of customized intervention to deal with the 'waves of dissonance or hatred' would more or less remain the same. The marginalities of asymmetric war zone at any point of the continuum, though relevant, cease to be the limiting factor.

APPENDIX - 1

INGREDIENTS OF OPERATIONAL PLAN

1. Validate Inputs:

- Analyze well.
- Verify as per need.
- Correlate with other details
- Magnify in terms of implication.
- Convert in actionable modules.

2. Study Area of Operation

- Geographical/topographical details on maps.
- Demographic/habitation details.
- Mapping of critical details.
  - Entry points.
  - Retreat/exit points.
  - Shelters/Camps of target groups.

- Ambush sites/ IED prone areas.
- Water points rivers/nallahs.
- Friendly/hostile habitation.
- Past incidents.
- Other crucial details.

- Demarcate core areas.

3. Determine Likely Duration of Ops Keeping in View

- Local terrain
- Entry and exit point distances.
- Travel mode/dropping and pickup points.
- Formats of tactical movements.
- Establishment of base camp.
- Strength and capability of target group.
- Various eventualities and intermittent halts.

4. Decide Configuration/Composition of Teams

- Number of teams.
- Selection of team leaders.
- Size of team.
- Composition.
- Quality of manpower.
- Support groups/squads.

5. Decide on Equipments and Weapons

- Scanning equipments.
- Detection/disposal equipments.
- Navigational aids.

- Fire power/area weapons/scale of ammunition.
- Protective gear/harnessing.
  - BP jackets.
  - Rain coats
  - Selection of shoes/uniform.
- Contingency kits.

6. Decide on Communication Needs

- HF/VHF/Sat phones/Cell phones/Head phones.
- Codes and passwords.
- Call signs and inter/intra group communication.
- Encryption needs.
- Link with Headquarters.
- Battery requirement.
- Contingency schemes

7. Decide on Transport

- Upto dropping point.
- From pick up point.

8. Decide on Rations

- Collective stock/Individual carry bag/Composite ration/ Traditional survival food.
- Type and quantity of ration.
- Energy booster/replenishers.
- Eating habits/plans and spacing between meals.
- Water purifier kits.
- Climate oriented supplements.
- Replenishment points, if any.

9. Integration/Interface With Other Forces

- Local guides/SPOs.
- Local sources.
- Local Police representative.
- Other Armed force in the area.

10. Medical Support

- Medical Kit.
- Life saving drugs.

11. Command Tools

- Detail programme sheet.
- Core area map.
- Communication processes.
- Evacuation plans.
- Retreat plan.
- Contingency management schemes.

12. Support System

- Heli support.
- UAV
- GPS

APPENDIX - 2

OPERATIONAL CHECK LISTS

1. Camp Security

1.1 Before Set Up

- Get full information about terrain, camp location, its vicinity, accessibility, nature of available accommodation and logistic supports.
- Seek general demographic details and list of reliable people.
- Collect details of various groups operating in the area and their bases and links as well as the modus operandi.
- Know past history of incidents of IED blasts in and around the location.
- Study existing security scenario and threat assessment.

- Develop rapport with SFs and police stations in proximity, establish connectivity and communication with them.

1.2 While Setting Up

- Dominate the area.
- Search and sensitize the area thoroughly from IEDs before occupying the site.
- Thoroughly search 200-300 mts area close to camp for IEDs/claymore mines.
- Look for wire, fresh dug surface, suspected objects on ground, trees or any such similar location.
- Ensure counter surveillance measure (the terrorists or their OGWs may start observing day-to-day activities from first day itself, they may be keen to know the camp layout).
- Ensure immediate security of the location by deploying sentries tactically.
- Plan layout of camp defense as well as the designs of morchas. Morcha on boundary wall needs to be slightly protruding outside so as to give visual cover alongside the wall. If necessary, observations posts should be at a height. A safe site can be planned.
- Place sentries and alarm posts, finalize illumination plan for night, decide requirement of various weapons and equipments at various sentry posts in day and night.
- Ensure communication between sentry posts and commander.
- Ensure adequate fortification of sentry post and watchtower. Locate signal centre and line tactically.

- While marking place for living and recreational areas, ensure contingency access to 'kote' and 'morchas' by troops. Design proper trenches or other covers for this purpose.
- Plan from enemy's perspective and simulate all possibilities.
- Define duties and beat of each sentry.
- Plan contingency of each layer of defence and each and every morcha/sentry.
- Conduct mock exercise to plug loopholes in security.
- Finalize siting of area weapons.
- Provide for nets or other covers in built-up areas to prevent grenade lobbying.

1.3 After Set Up

- Prepare comprehensive camp standing orders taking into consideration all possible operational and administrative tasks.
- Brief all men about security plan and their role.
- Explain the incident command chain.
- Finalize stand to drills.
- Plan for precautions against fire.
- Plan for contingency power supply.

1.4 Vehicle Security

- Proper security for vehicles inside the camp.
- Parking of vehicle should be away from the perimeter so that grenade attack cannot damage them.
- Vehicles should not be parked close to each other.
- Vehicles should not be parked in such a way that

it blocks the sight of view or line of fire, as per the scheme of camp defence.

- Ensure that vehicle fuel is not used to create a secondary blast.

1.5 Security in and Around Camp

- Visualize all possible exit/entry routes and control the access to camp. With neo-technology, one can also think of thermal imagers or CCTV coverage at vantage points.
- Dominate the areas in proximity of the camp tactically, so that the militants do not carry out surveillance or concentrate on camp attack.
- Conceptualize all possible ways of camp attack and prepare counter strategy.
- A quick reaction team should always be in readiness to counter any eventuality.
- Appropriate alarm system be in place to alert all sentries and other personnel in the camp about the danger.
- Contingency plans with neighbouring units should also be rehearsed, which may include cordoning the area, placing cut-offs, regulating traffic, etc.
- Create hurdles for intruders in approaching the camp entrance/perimeter. Use zig-zag mobile barriers/concertina wire/iron spikes/trenches with coverable planks or other methods which can be effective according to ground realities.
- Make trenches inside the camp for movement and taking position by the troopers.
- Clear trees around the camp in certain areas where they can give cover to attackers.

1.6 Security of Camp Against Night Attack

- Make approach access to the protected area very difficult.
- Ensure deployment of suitable guards at watch tower/on vantage locations around the periphery with night vision devices and sophisticated long range modern weapons.
- Provide adequate uninterrupted lighting in the periphery extending up to 100-200 meters around the periphery.
- The farthest 'light-exposed area' should be provided with intrusion alarm system, so that mass attack is detected from 100-200 meters which could be a safe distance to alert the entire camp.
- Check the preparedness of camp against mass attack equipped with hand grenades, patrol bomb or improved devices.
- Each camp should be in communication with 4-5 other strategic camps/police stations through a scrambled communication system.
- Since security involves physical action and alertness, duty hours should be rationalized

2. Operational Movement

2.1 Movement by Vehicles

- Decide on use of MPV, if available. So also decide on the use of Jammers in RCIED prone areas.
- As far as possible, keep vehicular movement to the minimum.
- Plan to use different routes for going and returning to the extent so possible.
- Routes could be changed frequently, so that no set

pattern is followed. Routes to be disclosed at the last moment.

- Avoid moving on routes which do not have alternate outlets. If there is suspicion of allurement or trap, move on foot tactically.
- Move preferably on metalled roads, even if it involves a longer route.
- Movement could be in groups of at least 2 to 3 vehicles, with irregular gaps within them.
- Sand bags may be placed on the floor of the vehicle to minimize the blast effect.
- Observe surrounding areas continuously for any suspicious activity or objects while moving.
- Minimize routine travel.
- Restricted/sudden drop in movement of civil vehicles or unscheduled shutting down of shops may be indicative of an imminent IED attack. Civilian strangers should not be given lift, as their dismounting point could be a potential ambush site.

2.2 Movement on Foot

- Use technical equipments for detection of IEDs as per the laid down drills with the help of scout party.
- Carry forest-clearing implements and navigate cross-country with the help of maps, compass, GPS etc.
- The beaten tracks need to be avoided.
- Patrols should move astride along the road and not on it.
- Conspicuous resting places like water point, good tree shade, etc., should be avoided.
- Bridges, culverts and fresh tracks leading to a bottle

neck or deliberately made to skirt around it, need to be searched carefully.

- Freshly dug and disturbed earth, dry grass, sticks, etc., need to be suspiciously scanned.
- Take help of sniffer dogs, if available.

2.3 Flanks With Formations

- Troops need to move tactically by adopting the necessary formation according to ground/terrain peculiarities.
- On being attacked, troops to immediately follow the established drill of 'dash down, crawl and observe'. Thereafter, appropriately retaliate with effective fire from flanks.
- While carrying out flanking attacks, troops could be in extended line so that the firing should not cause injury to own personnel.

2.4 Base

- All round defence and placement of weapons, particularly LMG/ Mortars etc. to be ensured.
- The base/camp should be in a position to retaliate effectively in case of any fire from the enemy.

2.5 Multiple Entry Points

- Multiple entry points may be decided on the basis of the ground situation and the requirement.
- This method is adopted to give a surprise to the enemy. Exact position and number of troops is made difficult to be assessed by the adversary.

2.6 Fire Control Orders

- Devise effective fire control drills within the party.
- Troops be in contact with commander through head

phones or other predetermined field signals.

- Rash and unplanned firing be avoided.
- Orders should be clear.

3. Safety Against Special Threats

3.1 Action on Finding Suspected IEDs

- Do no rush towards the suspected object.
- Survey surrounding area for the bomb/secondary device. Inform BD squad.
- Do not disturb the object.
- Explosive should be handled with caution, one should be especially careful while handling detonators.
- Carry buttressing, baffling and venting, if located within an enclosed space.
- Cordon off the area and evacuate people from its vicinity to prevent casualty in case of its explosion.

3.2 Search of a Place

- Lookout for recently disturbed area both outdoors and indoors.
- Search for sawdust, brick dust, wood chips, tin foils or greasy paper wrappings which could indicate presence of an IED.
- Locate 'out of place' objects which appear abnormal.
- Disturbed road carpeting or even freshly repaired roads to be viewed suspiciously.
- Partly open windows/doors/drawers could be booby traps.
- Fresh plaster/cement could be hiding an explosive device.

- Fish line and electric wires are likely components of an IED.
- Cut or trampled vegetation, crops could be camouflaging an IED.
- Dusty footprints to be studied carefully.
- Scorched or a newly painted spot could be indicative of covering the location of an IED.
- Freshly dug or filled areas may be tell-tale signs of a buried IED.

3.3 Car Bombs

- Parking regulations can effectively prevent vehicle bomb explosions in the vicinity of important buildings and strategic installations.
- Re-routing traffic permanently or temporarily can protect a specific target.
- Isolating parking lots in vulnerable areas by locating them at a safe distance can minimize the damage in case of an explosion.
- Security parking labels can ascertain the genuineness of the vehicle and its owner in protected areas.
- Radio frequency identification (RFID) technology can provide solutions for access control of vehicles at important places.
- The plan of movement of vulnerable persons, including security forces, needs to be kept absolutely secret.
- Regular movements that establish a pattern need to be avoided.
- Extensive use of sniffer dogs and metal/explosive detector, particularly in road opening and search operations is desirable.

- Any unusual happening should be taken as a warning.
- Unclaimed, unattended vehicle, two wheelers or any other movable object could be fitted with an explosive device. These should not be approached or touched without proper verification by experts.
- Patrol parties in built up areas must keep the area under observation from vantage points to spot unusual persons trying to park vehicles too close to the road or in crowded places.
- While carrying searches of suspected cars, the following should be looked at:
    - *Inside boot:* floor (especially the sides) and around the fuel tank.
    - *Interior:* underneath and behind the rear seats, underneath the front seat, beneath the mats/ carpets, armrests, dashboard including heater, air vent pipes, glove compartment, door cavities and inside fuel tank, etc.
    - *Engine compartment:* inside heater/air tubes, air filter, radiator and batteries.
    - *Exterior:* wheel hubs, under wheel arches, behind front grill and headlights, behind front and rear bumper.
    - *Underbody:* underneath the vehicle from all the sides and spare wheel, if fitted under rear of vehicle.
    - *Large box sections* or double skin areas of vehicles should be checked to find any modifications.

3.4 Human Bomb

- Site post/camp on a dominating ground, if possible, to have a natural advantage against militants.

- Place sentries/guards all around the perimeter.
- Field of view and field of fire must not be restricted by any natural or manmade obstructions.
- Restrict entry/exit points to gain a controlled access. One out of two gates at entrance should be a strong barrier.
- A bullet proof sentry post should be erected slightly away from the barrier. Sentry at main gate must be in pairs. One should check, frisk and the other should give him cover.
- Second sentry post should be built in the appropriate depth at such a place from where effective fire cover can be provided to the sentries at first sentry post.
- Security lights should be resorted to detect and provide difficult approach for the sneakers. These, in no case, should illuminate one's own vulnerable areas.
- Living accommodation should not be at one place but at different places all around the camp.
- All the personnel should keep their weapons round the clock.
- The post/camp should be divided into small pockets and junior commanders be nominated as pocket commanders, who will take control in the crisis situation.
- An effective local alarm system controlled by the second sentry post should be established which may alert troops in case of a crisis. Once alarm is sounded, personnel would not only protect themselves but also help in destroying the intruders as per the laid down drills.
- Quick Response Team (QRT) should always be available in the camp next to the inner sentry post

at entrance. QRT should be well trained in the crisis drill. Adequate rehearsals should be done to ensure quick and accurate action and to avoid chaos in a real crisis situation.

4. De-Briefing & Documentation

- Immediately on return from operation/movement, troops to reassemble.
- Weapons and equipments should be counted and checked for damage.
- Commanders to ensure the correct reporting.
- Commander to briefly recall and review the assigned task and planning.
- All deviations from plan to be discussed and analyzed.
- Good observations should be highlighted.
- The shortcomings and losses should be analyzed.
- Remedial actions should be clearly evolved and explained to all.
- The process of de-briefing should be properly documented for help in future.

5. Need for being Innovative

- The insurgents keep changing their tactics. It is increasingly imperative on the part of SFs to be innovative, to mitigate likely 'neo-threats' from adversaries.
- There cannot be any final word but one can cite a few examples for future leads:
- Use of local people, either those who are reliable or those who have been victims of terrorists, as special police officers to guide on the local terrain/

demography and also help in generating intelligence inputs.

- Use of local tools, equipment and vehicles as per the need, to traverse the area and neutralize the IEDs (e.g., tractor with land tillers helped digging out command wires hidden underneath the land alongside the road).
- Coinciding operations with socio-cultural events or climatic conditions.

Leading to Success in an Operation

Planning
↓
Briefing
↓
Monitoring
↓
Programme Implementing
↓
Retreating
↓
Debriefing
↓
Data Updating
↓
Plan Revision

APPENDIX - 3

CHECKLIST ON ADVANCED TACTICS

1. Preventive Security Drills

- Conduct threat and vulnerability analysis
- Make security plan keeping in view:
  - anti sabotage checks
  - access control procedures
  - anti subversion and identification processes
  - integrated and smart equipment systems as force multiplier
  - selection, training and deployment of reliable/ expert manpower
  - synergy with other administrative and operational agencies
  - public education and cooperation

- communication systems
- generation of databank and its analysis, house keeping
- parking area designs and safety norms
- emergency exits and safe holding areas
- digitalized maps for smooth navigation in crisis
- crisis management plans - threat calls/evacuation drills/medical emergency/personal security/ communication/information systems.

- Put security commander and his team in place and implement the plan
- Conduct security audit
- Security refinements, augmentation and training

2. Terrorist attack and hostage situation

- Conduct advance security and vulnerability analysis. Keep preventive security systems in place.
- Make state level, district level and micro level crisis management groups in advance with clear charter of duties and operational checklists.
- Put crisis management plan for each level in place covering following aspects-
  - cordoning and cutting off the area
  - interventions for release of hostages
  - neutralizing the terrorists
  - medical care and rehabilitation plans
  - public information and reporting systems
  - post incident investigations
- Activation of core groups and crisis control room in integrative manner.

- Establishing operational control room on the spot.
- Activating base camp adjoining control room for movement of required manpower, inventories and logistics.
- Enabling ATS/STF/expert groups to handle the situation and make necessary armed interventions in accordance with SOPs.
- Operationalize information and reporting systems.

3. Checklist for Communication Surveillance

- Develop expert personnel to perform these tasks
- Plan inventory profile
- Ensure legal compliances and necessary permissions
- Coordinate with service providers
- Follow laid down procedures and logging systems
- Keep record of each intervention and data generation
- Maintain secrecy of operations, follow safe procedures with controlled access
- Conduct internal security checks and audit, control deviations
- Plot the information on GTM & HTM database
- Pass on the analytical inputs to OPS teams in real time
- Ensure proper documentation

4. Technical possibilities in surveillance

- Collecting Data of all the calls coming or going through international gate-ways.
- Scanning of local numbers constantly in contact with given international numbers.

- Study of call details of local numbers.
- Verification of local numbers physically on ground to ensure if their activities are suspicious.
- Putting verified suspicious numbers on parallel listening watch.
- Scanning of numbers supplied by other agencies.
- Seek data from international gate-ways of telephone lines regarding incoming & outgoing calls by satellite phones.
- Constant monitoring of different organizations, which are not banned but are sympathizers of terror outfits.

5. Electronic Surveillance and its domain

- Digital data and data flow through radio access
- Landline phones, mobile phones, satellite phones, internet services
- Broader perspective: online banking, booking and similar transactions

(A) Off line phones: CDR (Call Data Record)/Log

- usage pattern
- contacted entities
- location
- handset identity
- certain switching parameters

(B) Off Line Internet: Log/Transaction history

- IP address/date/time–unique entity for connecting to a server
- Inbox/outbox/address book/ draft, etc., of target ID

- Bank transaction logs - Branch/ ATM/POS (Point of Sale)
- Credit card usage history /PNP (Person Not Present) usage–earlier main source of fraud but plugged by 3D security

(C) Online interception: as per the laid down procedure

- Interception of landline/mobile/mail ID:
- Sec 5(2) of Indian Telephone Act empowers to intercept on the basis of 5 criteria, the most widely used is to pre-empt a criminal act.
- Interception orders are issued by Government/ Home Secretary.
- Department of Telecom/TRAI (Telecom Regulatory Authority of India), Ministry of Information Technology (for mail interception) has issued guidelines.
- There are also various types of online alerts for tracking online banking and debit/credit/ATM card transactions.
- IT Act 2000 (Amendments in 2009) has widened the ambit of handling cyber crime through mobile device and computer.
- Forensic science is used to produce piece of evidence in the court of law to support investigations.

Appendix - 4

Ops Analysis Profile (Decision Support System Tool)

1. Highlights on aims and policy issues of target groups.

2. Intensity of violence:

- Overall violent activities/violence level over a period.
- Target group, initiated violence and impact. Intelligence correlation.
- SF initiated violence and impact.
- Pattern of targeting. Victim analysis.
- Geographical spread analysis.
- Elimination/neutralization of target groups - quantum and seizures - area wise break up - comparison of concentration pockets and SF actions in terms of area results.

- Neutralizations of top leaders/commanders.
- SF killed in action - attrition ratio in terms of SF killed and target group killed - reasons for casualties.
- Civilian fatalities - level of fatalities over a period of time-area wise fatalities - special segments like minorities- incidental fatalities - terror quotient.
- Number of direct attacks, IED blasts, other forms of violence.
- Analysis by type of IEDs and area of usage.
- Incidents of stand-off fire and impact analysis in terms of victims, area of occurrence besides time pattern.
- Suicide bombers and car bomb cases: numbers, impact, area, timing and techniques.
- Weapon snatching from SFs.

3. Apprehensions and surrenders

- Apprehensions over a period of time, area wise analysis (AWA), seizure of arms/equipments.
- Comparison of AWA with known concentration pockets.
- Surrenders - periodicity, numbers, area wise analysis, motive, arms and equipments.

4. Target group strength and concentration

- Periodical known strength-group wise - changes over a period.
- Group wise areas of concentration - further spread or reduction.
- Comparison including figures of recruitment, infiltration/exfiltration, liquidations and neutralizations.
- Comments on various trends and implications

5. Status of infrastructure of target groups and changes therein:

Training Camps	-	Number, locations, strength, comparison over a period, outcome of camps raided/ destroyed.
Type of training	-	Nature of tactics, new drills, new technological induction, arms, terrain navigation, etc. Analysis of training material seized.
Military capabilities	-	Changes in militancy structure, fire power and other striking capabilities.
Intelligence Mechanism	-	Intelligence mechanism of the target group, varied modus operandi.
Communication	-	Up-gradation of equipment, new methodologies, codes and signals, interception details, encryption modules, information couriers, communication equipments.
	-	Comments on various trends and implications.

6. Networking support

- Networking agents/organizations/OGWs.
- Type of support.
- Modus operandi of networking agents.
- Environmental factors promoting such associations/ affiliations.
- Identification of and action against frontal organizations /OGWs.
- NGO networking trends. Sub-continental links.

7. Recruitments, infiltration, and exfiltration:

- Areas of recruitments, number of recruitments, changes in recruitment volumes over a period, nature of affected population, inducements for induction, etc.
- Number of infiltration, changes over a period, infiltration routes, source states/areas, timing of infiltration, MO of infiltration, size of groups infiltrating, arms and equipments with infiltrators, creation of shallow dumps as conduits, encounters with forces.
- Comments on various trends and implications.

8. Funding

- Quantum of fund flows over a period. Funds' profiling.
- Group wise receipt of funds.
- Funds parking.
- MO of fund collection/extortions.
- Fake currency circulation.
- Increasing/decreasing trends with plausible reasons.
- Implications for future.

9. Attitude of civil population

- General attitude.
- Strong holds of sympathizers, shelterers and reasons.
- Movement routes though various habitations.
- Impact of SF action on people. Support to target groups.

- OGW support structure - number/quantum and region wise spread, nature/type of people involved, change in OGW configuration.
- Aspects meriting attention with respect to SF and public relationship/partnership.

10. Political and Subversive activities by target groups

- Mobilization of masses and their response.
- Links with political parties, direct/indirect participation.
- Propaganda/subversion through frontal organi-zations/NGOs.
- Infiltration in Government, social institutions.
- Nature of separatist groups.
- Inter-group rivalries.

11. Perception management by target groups

- Press and Media.
- Cyber network.
- Literature and publicity material.
- Public meetings
- Assistance to local populace.

12. Major developments in the area

- Special governmental measures.
- Initiatives by the local police and other forces. Presence of various forces in the area.
- Synergetic advantages, if any, including developmental activities.
- Perception management by government, security forces.

- Mobilization of people's support.
- Policy on surrender.

13. Summary of overall trends:

- Aims and policy issues of target groups.
- Target group infrastructure.
- Communication network.
- Strength and spread, sensitive pockets.
- Training and preparedness.
- Stock and dumps of arms.
- Funding and fund parking.
- Trends in violence.
- Morale of target group.
- Engineered subversions and overt public protests.

14. Future assessment:

- On level of violence.
- On support base of target groups.
- Likely change in tactics.
- On change in size and spread.
- On action against security forces, government establishments, VIPs.
- On socio-political scenario in the area of operation.

15. Recommended Policy Initiatives:

- SF deployment grids.
- SF quality up gradation.
- SF morale enhancement.
- Strengthening logistical supports.
- Inter-institutional synergy.

- Security linked developmental issues.
- Perception management.
- Various licensing systems.
- Government beneficiaries' network.
- Economic enforcement network.
- Action plan.

Glossary

Agent. A full time intelligence functionary put on the payroll for performing an assigned task in the domain of the adversary. An agent can be introduced in the system of the adversary or his own functionaries and may be won over. They generally work under cover.

AOR. Area of responsibility flowing from a given grid deployment.

Area Domination. A process of operational exercises, not only to acquaint well with the local geographical as well as human terrain, but also to secure tactical advantage over the adversary. It is carried with well-defined objectives and proper cost-benefit, risk analysis.

Asset. In the field of intelligence, an asset is a source who has been critically tested over a period of time and then enlisted for fetching various inputs required to gain operational edge over the adversary.

Asymmetric Warfare. Conflict situation where unconventional methods are used to exploit the weakness of the other in order to mitigate the deficiencies in quantity or quality of resources; as contrary to direct military action.

Blind Self. A person is said to be in a blind self-mode if he has not discovered himself well in terms of his thoughts, cognitions, values, and such similar factors which determine his internal configuration, besides his being equally ignorant about the other person with whom he is interacting.

BDDS. Stands for Bomb Detection and Disposal Squad, a team of experts duly trained, equipped and motivated to undertake the designated tasks as above.

Cafetarian approach. Choice of options given to the beneficiary under the scheme to make it more acceptable and congruent with person specific or situation specific requirements.

Chemiluminescence. Emission of light, with little heat, as a result of chemical reaction.

Car bombs. Improvised explosive device placed in a car, or other vehicle meant for detonation and explosion. It can carry heavy explosive material and damage large buildings and properties. The fuel tank provides a secondary explosion.

CATS. A covert operational group consisting of underground elements used by authorities in the counter insurgency offensives, which may not be otherwise having any legal sanctity.

CBRNE. Device combining chemical, biological, radiological, nuclear agents with conventional explosives. It is an enhanced threat.

CGRL. Carl Gustav Rocket Launcher is a man portable recoilless anti tank weapon with varied purpose ammunitions.

Civic action programme. Long or short term projects of community welfare conducted through the capabilities and the resources of security forces, as part of goodwill mission during operations.

Cognitive damage. Disruptions caused to the ways a person can view certain given phenomenon; deflecting the capacity to perceive from a given angle.

Collateral damage. Incidental damage during a combat.

Combing. Systematic point-to-point search of an area with due precautions.

Community Policing. Participative approach to policing where community members are appropriately integrated with the local police. Under such a system, open-collaborative modules are worked out within the police domains where problem- identification is followed by proactive problem solving. Formats may differ from place to place and situation to situation. Civic action programs may be evolved to build mutual confidence and synergy, tailored to the needs of the local populace.

Compact Revolutionary Zone. The red corridor in East of India, consisting of certain portions of AP, Bihar, Chattisgarh, Jharkhand, Karnataka, Orissa, West Bengal, MP and UP, witnessing acute Maoist violence.

Cost-benefit analysis. Comparative analysis of the benefits and the corresponding costs of given decisions on various parameters, including the time scale.

Counter IED. The measures adopted to neutralize, counter the IED threats.

Counter Insurgency Grids. The demarcated areas, based on GTM as well as HTM, where counter insurgency operations could be optimally launched by the designated security set up.

Counter Intelligence. Efforts made by intelligence agencies to thwart the attempts by other agencies, adversaries to collect intelligence against them.

Covert operations. Clandestine operations launched against the adversary.

Customised Solutions. Situation/person/place specific modulations in the problem solution domains carried out to optimize the performance .

Dalam. A group of Naxal activist at the cutting edge level.

Demonstration effect. The impact of a higher order entity on the behaviour or the emulation pattern of those under it; the effect a senior or superior carries on his juniors or followers as emanating from his conduct.

Dirty Bomb. Bomb or weapon that combines radioactive material with conventional explosives.

DTMF. Dual tone multi frequency signaling used in voice frequency bands for switch over.

Fidayeen attack. Though the word fidayeen stands for self sacrifice, the term as a whole is used for a suicide bomber who is ready to kill himself, intends to kill others and cause vast damage.

Force Multiplier. The technical and infrastructural support systems that enhance the efficiency of the security forces such that well equipped personnel in lesser strength deliver greater results than the groups of larger strength could otherwise do.

Frontal organizations. The organizations active in public domain to espouse the cause of the underground elements. They play a major role in perception management and opinion building. They operate within the acceptable norms so as to escape the 'legal – clutches' and yet provide plausible support to the outlaws.

Geographical Terrain Mapping. GTM connotes the system of assimilation and integration of geographical data and presenting them in a format that could be relevant for the operational success.

Grid deployment. Cogent demarcation of the geographical area amidst the security forces for optimizing the operational performance with a due sense of responsibility.

Goal displacement. Distortions leading to compromise in the objectives set for normative performance.

GPS. Global positioning system is a space based, global navigation satellite system which provides reliable location and time information.

Guerilla Zones. Targeted areas for guerilla warfare.

HMTD. Hexamythelene triperoxide diamine – a high explosive organic compound used as primary explosive in mining.

Homeostatic response. A Management terminology, which indicates the capacity of a system to recoup itself and regains its original response capacity to the extent possible.

Human Intelligence. Intelligence gathered through human beings, which may be a contact, source or agent.

Human Terrain Mapping. HTM connotes the system of getting appropriate understanding of local culture and social structures for improving operational effectiveness. It is basically getting better insight into the local populace. It focuses more on 'who the enemy is not', rather than knowing 'who the enemy' is. So much so, it differs from the traditional intelligent system.

Hypergolic. Having, the propensity of spontaneous ignition.

IED. Improvised explosive device is a bomb fabricated in an improvised manner and purported to cause the desired destruction.

Interactive learning. A style of learning arousal through mutual interaction and appreciation. It is a multi pronged flexible approach as against one-way flow of inputs where stimulus – response patterns are rigid and compartmentalized. Secondly, real time feedback is available under interactive learning.

Infiltration. Sneaking across a border, making clandestine entry in the domain of the opposing party.

Information warfare. Connotes war of information to draw tactical advantage. It may take the shape of any manipulation, distorted propagation or otherwise. It may be used as a psychological warfare tool.

Jungle warfare. Operational engagement by security forces in jungle terrain. It involves a set of techniques for combat and sustenance in forested area.

Learning Curve. The rate of adoption, sustenance and decline in behavioural response/level of skills, when subjected to a set of stimulators and the reinforcers, subject to the individual variants.

Liberated area. A term used by Naxalities for an area where they claim to neutralize the governmental systems and establish their own hold.

Line Functionaries. A management term used for cutting edge level ground functionaries.

Low Intensity Conflict. The conflict situation where armed forces are deployed selectively with adequate restraint in order to control the defiant groups and get them back to the main stream.

Masking. Covering an activity under a different label. Doing an act keeping someone else in the forefront, so as to hide one's own identity. The technique is often used for various intelligence/psychological operations.

Money Laundering. Any technique to conceal illegally gained money and adoption of such methods which may give it a different colour and shade.

MPV. Stands for Mine Protected Vehicle – an armoured personnel carrier – provides defense against sharpnels and ambushes – depending upon the configuration. It also grants protection against landmines.

Multiple Intrusion Techniques. Techniques to enter into an area with tactical modules that grant maximum possible coverage and dominance.

Narco terrorism. Terrorist acts thriving on funds raised through narco trafficking-use of narco trafficking funds to boost terrorism and launch offensives against the government, enforcement agencies.

Naxalism. Left radical Communism, supportive of Maoist political sentiments and ideology, emanating from Naxalbadi, a village in West Bengal. Later spread to other areas facing splits and mergers.

Negative Entropy. Characteristic of a system of delivering comparatively lesser output than the inputs, thereby consuming certain inputs for self sustenance.

OGW. Open ground workers who, prima-facie, live as law abiding citizens but clandestinely provide logistical support to the outlaws indulging in militancy, insurgency or terrorism.

Open Self. A person is said to be in an open self mode when he knows himself as well as the other person, with whom he is interacting, well enough in terms of all the factors constituting the internal configuration of one's personality.

Opportunity cost. Gains from the other options foregone vis-a-vis the option adopted under the given circumstances.

PDA. Personal digital assistant also known as palm top computer, is a mobile device with internet connectivity, electronic visual display and acts as personal information manager.

Perception Management. Ways and means to influence the cognitions, thought processes and 'logic ' domains of an individual such that he grasps and comprehends a practical phenomenon as desired by the stimulator, and as manipulated through the well calibrated re-inforcers.

PFNA. Perfluorononanoic acid of synthetic nature that is also an environmental contaminant.

PETN. Pentaerythrito teranitrate – mixed with plasticizer to form a plastic explosive.

PLGA. Here it refers to the main operational/fighting segment of Naxals known as People's Liberation Guerrilla Army.

Photoluminescence. Emission of light through excitation of photons.

Proxy war. The warfare in which opposing powers use third parties as substitutive fighting elements.

Psychological Warfare. Planned operations to disseminate selective information, which can influence cognitions and perceptions of the target population, thereby modulating their thinking and response patterns. Purpose is to induce them to behave in a fashion, which is congruent to the objectives of the perpetuator.

QRTs. Quick Reaction Terms are well configured and well equipped, highly motivated small compact groups to face any emergent crisis situation.

RCIED. Radio Controlled Improvised Explosive Device.

RDX. Research Department Explosive: While, crystalline solid – chemically known as cyclo trimethylene trinitramine – one of the powerful high explosive.

Response Capacity Deficit. RCD concept helps in identifying the difference between optimal desired response and the actual response. The deficit analysis indicates the cause and effect relationship useful for improvising the quality of the performance.

Role Displacement. Deflection from the original role/ responsibility arising due to the extraneous factors, more of a perceptional incongruency.

Role Model. A personality par excellence for emulation by others. This may, however, be situation and place specific.

Risk Analysis. Identification and assessment of factor, which may hamper the success of a mission. This may involve correlation of various vectors inter-se and study the impact in terms of time, quality, quantity or other criticalities.

ROP Road opening parties are the advance teams sent to sanitise the routes and the nearby potential area before the main contingents move out. This is to prevent the casualties owing to any IED, ambush or such similar tactics adopted by the advarsary.

Sleeper Cell. A hidden or covert group nurtured in a fashion that it can effectively resist the invasion by the opposing organization. It can organize counter offensives. It lies dormant until activated.

Suicide Bomber. An attack through a human bomb, a suicidal act intended for homicide bombing and to inflict wide spread damage.

SF. Stands for Security Forces, in particular the armed forces of the central/federal governments.

SOP. Standard operating procedures devised for operations so as to minimize errors and enhance quality of the output.

SPO. Special police officers are the selected citizens from the local community mobilized to assist the police in operational tasks. Legal provisions to this effect exist in the Police Act.

SWOT. Management tool to analyze strength, weakness, opportunity and threats. This facilitates situational analysis for the purpose of locating the best possible option at any given point of time.

Subversion. An act of throwing off those in the establishment; aborting the system.

Sabotage. A deliberate action, in a concealed manner, to disrupt another entity.

SEMTEX. High powered plastic explosive made with the combination of PETN and RDX.

SOG. Special Operation Group configured, equipped and tasked to perform given missions.

Source Handler. The person who is adept in handling a source (asset) and getting the required performance through him in the field of intelligence collection, covering all risks and obstacles which may generally arise in this game.

Spying. Collecting information of a secret nature without the knowledge or permission of the possessor of such information. It is a clandestine operation, mostly institutional in nature.

STF. Special Task Force raised to perform highly specialized jobs in an operational environment. They are raised, trained, equipped and motivated for stressful situations.

Sub optima. Compromised or constrained solution domains providing lesser than optimum output.

Surrogate bases. Substitutive base to operate from, under different identity. It could also mean emulated response base.

TATP. Acetone peroxide – an organic peroxide – white crystalline powder with acrid odour – a primary high explosive.

Technical Intelligence. Intelligence collected through the monitoring of communication equipments, using means of electronic surveillance and cyber surfing or other gadget based interceptions.

Thermo Redox. It is an explosive trace detection technology based on decomposition of an explosive substance.

Third eye. Generally used for intelligence tasks which are mostly covert.

TNT. Trinitrotoluene - a yellow coloured solid – used as explosive – has high activation energy – widely used with ammonium nitrate.

TOVEX. Water gel explosive composed of ammonium nitrate and methyl ammonium nitrate – used by oil companies – as a replacement for dynamite.

UAV. Unmanned Aerial Vehicle used in operations with various scanning equipments of different payloads in order to capture terrain details. Could be used for other purposes as per the objectives of the navigator.

Ulterior transaction. The hidden communication purported to achieve a different result than what it apparently reflects.

Unified Command. The Command and control system put in use to synergize the functioning of multiple agencies on a conflict grid.

Urban Warfare. A combat in towns and cities, i.e. urban area.

VDS. Village defense societies are formed as part of community policing in rural areas with varied modules, primarily for village security.

Victim Reassurance Programmes. Programmes launched by the government towards compensation, rehabilitation and settlement of the victims of insurgency and all those who want to join back into the social mainstream.

War of Perceptions. Various communication modules adopted to influence the psyche of the masses and generate such perceptions which may put the players in the game at a tactical advantage over the other. It leads to greater psychological victory than otherwise achieved through war of guns. After all, local populace is at the base whose support is ever essential.

Window dressing. Patching up a situation to hide certain deficits, so as to showcase a better picture than the real.

Zeroing. Narrowing down on the precise target point/ pinpointing on the zone of success, taking into account the individual specifics.

Zero Tolerance. A performance yardstick where no deviation from the norms is acceptable.

Bibliography

Books

Bernard Brodie, *War and Politics,* New York, Mac Millan,1973.

Burns T and G Stalker, *The Management of Innovations,* London; Tavistock.

Faultlines, Vol18, The Institute for Conflict Management, writings of Ajay Sahai and KPS Gill, Bulwark Books, 2007.

Gill KPS, *Terror and Containment Perspectives of India's Internal Securinty,* Gyan Publishing House, New Delhi, 2001.

Harry Eekstein, *Internal War, Problems and Approaches,* Glenco: The Free Press, 1964.

Hazarika Sanjoy, *Strangers of the Mist,* Penguins, NewDehi -1994.

Mitra DM, *The Litort Papers; Understanding Indian Insurgencies*; US Army War College 2007.

Raman B; *Terrorism, Yesterday, Today and Tomorrow*, Lancers, NewDelhi, 2008.

Saikia Jaideep and Steponova Ekaterina; *Terrorism: Patterns of Internationalisation*; Sage, New Delhi; 2009.

Singh Prakash, *The Naxalite Movement in India*, Rupa, NewDelhi, 1995.

Smith Paul Jr, *Terrorism and Violence in Southeast Asia*, Eastgate Books, New York, 2005.

SunTzu, *The Art of War*, ©1981 James Clavell, Hodder and Stonghton Ltd, London, 2006.

Websites

http://en.wikipedia.org/wiki/Main_Page

http://www.au.af.mil/au/awc/awcgate/milreview/ancker.pdf

http:/www.highbeam.com/doc/1G1-177589366.html http:/www mha.nic.in/docs/CIVICACTIONPROGRAMME

www.wood.army.mil/mpbulletin/pdfs/april%2006/mott.pdf

www.scribd.com/.../Concept-of-Operations-for-Police-Intelligence-Operations

Published Articles

[SELF]

- Society must have vision for its policing, *Hindustan Times*, Lucknow, May, 2010.
- Operation Aman, *National Police Academy Journal*, Dec., 2007.
- Stress Management in Internal Security Forces, ibid.

- Inter personal relations inter-se the Commander and the troopers; *CRPF News*, March, 2007.
- Terror in age of technology, *The Black Cat (NSG)*, 2007.
- Pushing up police professionals on human rights index (HRI); *CRPF News*, April, 2007.
- Fight against the invisible–from operations to perceptions, *CRPF News*, Nov., 2006.
- Welfare of Central Police Forces; certain inherent issues based on neo formats.
- Police modernizations schemes –an impact analysis, *CRPF News*, 2005.
- Growing organisations: The art of image building, *Indian Police Journal*, 2005.
- Human Terrain Mapping to check conflicts, ibid, 2008.
- Managing low intensity conflicts, *Asia Defence News*, Sept., 2008.
- Managing Risks, *FORCE*, vol 5, No. 7, March, 2008.
- Building a secured future, *The Black Cat (NSG), Journal*, 2005.
- Ever fighting men, *National Police Academy Journal*, Dec., 2002.
- Policing the Policeman's Belly, *Hindustan Times, Lucknow*, Oct., 28, 2001.
- Men in Khaki get the blues, *Hindustan Times, Lucknow*, Aug., 5, 2001.
- Crisis of Policing in India, *Indian Police Journal*, Sept., 2001.
- Challenges before the Police, *The Times of India*, Lucknow, Dec., 07, 1998.

ANONYMOUS

THAT IMAGINATION IS STRONGER THAN KNOWLEDGE;
THAT MYTH IS MORE POTENT THAN HISTORY;
THAT LAUGHTER IS THE ONLY CURE FOR GRIEF;
THAT DREAMS ARE MORE POWERFUL THAN FACTS;
THAT THOSE WHO ARE BLINDED BY AMBITION SEE EVEN LESS THAN THOSE BLIND SINCE BIRTH;
THAT A SENSE OF BELONGING FAR OUTWEIGHS MATERIAL LONGING TOWARDS ACHIEVING HAPPINESS;
THAT FAITH ALWAYS TRIUMPHS OVER EXPERIENCE;
THAT RESILIENCE CAN OVERCOME BRILLIANCE;
AND I HOLD THE CONVICTION THAT YOU CANNOT CHOOSE YOUR BATTLEFIELD – THE GODS DO THAT FOR YOU.

INDEX